What people are

Sea Serpents: Or
British Col

What, if anything, is the perplexing sea monster known as Cadborosaurus? Join Pat Spain as he combines adventure travelogue and behind-the-scenes insight from TV-land with the wiley investigative powers of a passionate naturalist and scientist. The right mix of hilariously funny anecdotes, a deep interest in the natural world, and a quest for mystery animals. **Dr. Darren Naish**, author of *Hunting Monsters: Cryptozoology and the Reality Behind the Myths*

When it comes to peering beyond the periphery of what is known to science, it's hard to imagine a better guide than Pat Spain. By his own happy admission an overgrown "weirdo adventure nature kid," now occupying the same body as a proper marine biologist, his approach to cryptozoology is both fun and serious, and built on a solid foundation of the non-crypto variety. As lively and up-for-anything on the page as he is on the screen, he also gives a bonus glimpse into the world of costume malfunctions and boiling swimming pools that exists behind the scenes of natural history TV.
**Jeremy Wade**, host of *River Monsters* and author of *How to Think Like a Fish*

Pat Spain is that rare thing; a rationalist who still embraces the possible and knows that there are more things in heaven and Earth than are dreamt of. A grown-up who has lost none of the childhood wonder and curiosity that makes the world magical. A scientist who keeps an open mind and rejoices in the fact that absence of proof is not proof of absence. There is nobody I'd want to travel with more to explore the wild side of our literally extraordinary planet. Buckle up and prepare for adventures.

**Harry Marshall**, Chairman and Co-Founder of Icon Films

# Sea Serpents: On the Hunt in British Columbia

or, How I Went to the Bottom of the Ocean, and a Giant Fish Accidentally got Me Drunk

## Titles in the On the Hunt series

# Sea Serpents: On the Hunt in British Columbia

or, How I Went to the Bottom of the Ocean, and a Giant Fish Accidentally got Me Drunk

Pat Spain

6TH
BOOKS

Winchester, UK
Washington, USA

JOHN HUNT PUBLISHING

First published by Sixth Books, 2022
Sixth Books is an imprint of John Hunt Publishing Ltd., No. 3 East St., Alresford,
Hampshire SO24 9EE, UK
office@jhpbooks.com
www.johnhuntpublishing.com
www.6th-books.com

For distributor details and how to order please visit the 'Ordering' section on our website.

ISBN: 978 1 78904 654 0
978 1 78904 655 7 (ebook)
Library of Congress Control Number: 2021942787

A CIP catalogue record for this book is available from the British Library.

Design: Stuart Davies

UK: Printed and bound by CPI Group (UK) Ltd, Croydon, CR0 4YY
Printed in North America by CPI GPS partners

We operate a distinctive and ethical publishing philosophy in
all areas of our business, from our global network of authors to
production and worldwide distribution.

# Contents

This book is for my parents, Maribeth and Al Spain, who simultaneously pushed me to challenge myself and made me secure in the person I am. They also sparked and fostered my enduring and consuming love of the ocean and its mysteries. The sea will always remind me of my parents' unconditional love.

# Introduction

Some of you may know me as the "(almost) King of the Jungle," "Legend Hunter," "that animal guy," "Beast Hunter" or "that guy who had cancer and catches snakes." Probably not, though. Despite having a couple of dozen hours of international TV series to my name, and giving hundreds of talks and presentations, I don't really get recognized very often – unless we're talking about college kids in Guwahati, India, middle-aged men in the US, or pre-teen Indonesian girls. My key demographics, it turns out. I struggle to name anything those groups have in common, besides me.

I left my home in Upstate New York at 16 to live in a barn in southern Maine for a marine biology internship, and I haven't stopped exploring since. My passion for wildlife led me to create my own YouTube-based wildlife series in 2004 and has landed me spots on Animal Planet, Nat Geo, Nat Geo Wild, Travel Channel, SyFy, BBC and more. Half of the TV shows I've made have never seen the light of day, but they were all an adventure and there isn't a single one I wouldn't do again if given the chance. Besides TV, I work full time in biotech, which is its own sort of adventure – albeit one where drinking the water is generally safer. I've been bitten and stung by just about everything you can think of – from rattlesnakes and black bears to bullet ants and a rabid raccoon – and I've lost count of the number of countries I've been to.

I've had the opportunity to travel the world, interacting with some of the strangest and rarest animals, while having the honor of living with indigenous peoples in some of the most remote locations – participating in their rituals, eating traditional meals, and massively embarrassing myself while always trying to remain respectful. I am a perpetual fish out of water, even in my home state of Massachusetts. This book is

1

part of the "On the Hunt" series, in which I get to tell some of my favorite stories from those travels.

This particular book is about my time in British Columbia in Canada, searching for the truth behind the mythical sea serpent Caddy with my friends while making an episode of the National Geographic channel series *Beast Hunter*, also called *Beast Man* in the UK, "Breast Hunter" by my wife, and "Beast Master" by almost everyone who meets me for the first time and tells me they enjoyed the series.

BC is beautiful. Everyone who has been there will tell you this. But it really is shockingly, painfully beautiful – stunning and breathtaking. It's like if coastal Maine and Big Sur had a baby. And it's populated by Canadians, who are just the best. God, Canadians are nice. Please take the attempts at humor in the following pages for what they are and know that I mean no disrespect. I hope you enjoy this book. If you do, please pick up the others from this series. If you don't, I'll probably hear about why on social media. Either way, thanks for reading!

## A disclaimer

My dog Daisy was the best. She loved hanging out in the backyard with my sister, Sarah, and me when we were playing hide-and-go-seek, catching bugs, or looking for arrow heads on the trails behind our house in Upstate NY. She would wait patiently at the base of any tree we climbed and chase away our neighbor's super scary dog (he ate a kitten once). She would also stand guard while I waited for the spider to crawl out of a crack in our chipped blue bulkhead cellar doors. It was huge, with green-metallic colored fur and red eyes, and Daisy would growl if I put my hand too close to it. She was a white poodle mix with poofy fur and perpetually muddy feet. Also, Daisy could fly, sometimes wore a cape, and would occasionally speak with a Southern drawl.

I don't have schizophrenia and Daisy was not an imaginary

friend – but she also didn't really exist. Despite never owning a dog as a child, I have honest, distinct memories of Daisy. Memories that go well beyond the stories my mom used to tell my sister and me about Daisy saving us from one tragedy or another. I also have detailed memories of being terrified, like heart-racing, nearly in tears fear the time Cookie Monster stole our shoes while we were wading in the creek catching crayfish and pollywogs. He would only give them back when we had the Count (who smelled like toothpaste) help us negotiate how many cookies it would take for each shoe, shoelace, and sock. Daisy ran back and forth from our house bringing with her a ransom of the ever-increasing number of chocolate chip cookies that my mom had left out to cool. The monster (I think people forget he is a monster by definition) kept finding loopholes in our deals, and the tension was getting higher and higher as the water rose in the creek. Cookie Monster smelled like BO and his eyes rolled around like a crazy person's. He was unstable. In the end, Daisy came through, as she always did.

Mom would start these stories "When you were both very small, we had a wonderful dog named Daisy," and they quickly took on a life of their own. They eventually made their way into our collective consciousness as real events, complete with details not included in the original stories which must have been added by Sarah and me. It was years later, during some holiday involving drinking (see "every holiday"), that we started reminiscing about childhood memories and one of us asked: "Did we really have a dog when we were little? I kind of feel like we did, but I also can't picture us having a dog with all of the other animals we had. Daisy, maybe?" It wasn't until then that we realized these were, in fact, fictitious stories our mom had made up to keep us entertained on rainy days in our old house. Stories that drew on real events (being terrorized by a neighbor's dog, getting stuck in a creek, finding snakes, spiders, and arrowheads, etc.), with Daisy taking the place of our mother as the heroine.

I guess what I mean by this is, all of the stories in this book are exactly how I remember them, but I honestly remember having a flying southern-belle dog and interacting with Muppets. Take that how you want. I had a great childhood.

Oh, also – All views expressed are my own and do not reflect those of National Geographic, The National Geographic Channel, Icon Films, John Hunt Publishing, or any other person or organization mentioned (or not mentioned) in this book.

## Chapter 1

# Why Yes, I Have Eaten Coconut M&Ms on the Bottom of the Ocean

I'm proud to say that I'm a huge marine biology nerd. I taught myself how to make the word "bio" by interlocking the fingers of my right hand, thereby creating the dorkiest gang sign of all time. I've been known to order seafood using binomial nomenclature, and once made a pilgrimage to the Delmarva Peninsula to observe the horseshoe crab mating season in person. Ben, the episode producer of the Canada episode, has also made the trek to Delmarva, but he was paid to document the unearthly sight that is a *Limulus* orgy. I did it because horseshoe crabs are awesome.

For the first time since graduating from college in 2002, I would have the opportunity to actually use my "marine biology" degree. I put "marine biology" in quotes because that is not what my degree is in. I received a degree in biology with a "parenthetical marine focus" – which does not appear, even in parentheses, anywhere on my degree, but was explained to me by my university to be there "in spirit." Just to clarify – they told me that "the spirit of your degree has a parenthetical marine focus." I was as confused as you are, both by that choice of wording and in finding out one month before graduating that the marine-biology program I was enrolled in had unfortunately been disbanded at some point and shifted to a "Marine Concentration," and no one had told me. I took marine biology classes, wrote my thesis on oysters, and did everything else needed to have a marine-biology degree – but, my degree officially says, in very large letters, "Bachelor of Science," in smaller letters "Cum Laude," and then in the smallest font on the degree "Biology." But here I was, about to put that degree to good use and track down a legendary sea serpent! Like so many (marine) biologists before me.

I would be heading to British Columbia to host an episode of *Beast Hunter* – a TV series produced by Icon Films for the National Geographic Channel – searching for the truth behind the legend of the mythical sea serpent Caddy. Someone on the production team let it slip that they were kicking around the idea of contracting a three-man submersible to bring us 1,000 feet down in the Agamemnon Channel off Canada's Sunshine Coast, at which my (marine) bio nerd-dom kicked into full gear, and I latched onto it with an annoyingly childlike persistence.

After making the initial suggestion and seeing my zeal for it, our production team started back peddling and my obsessive and immature promises truly started to rival those of an eight-year-old attempting to convince their parents to get a Newfoundland puppy.

"It's too expensive," they said.

"I'll sleep in the car and eat nothing but power bars, which I'll provide for the whole crew, for the entire shoot, to save money," I said.

"We'll be cutting it really close schedule-wise."

"I will personally drive insanely and illegally fast to make up for lost time."

"It's a three-man sub. Who's going to check audio, lighting, script points, operate the equipment, etc., when we've got you and the pilot taking up two-thirds of the spots?

"I will film myself, mic myself, test sound, regulate the light, and get every single shot correct on the first take."

"What if we don't see anything great?"

"1,000 feet down is such a bizarre world that anything we see will constitute the greatest shot in the episode, unless a sea serpent headbutts the camera in a different scene."

"Pat, I really don't know. It sounds amazing, but I'm just not sure we can commit to that kind of expenditure."

"PLEASE, PLEASE, PLEASE, PLEASE, PLEASE. I promise I'll do anything you want, for ever! ANYTHING. You name it! I won't complain about anything ever again! I'll carry all of the equipment on every shoot we ever do. PLEASE! I'll never ask for anything else again!"

I finally wore them down and the contract was signed, possibly just to get me to shut up about it. We would have to cut the budget on other episodes, and I may need to spend a few weeks of my life as the personal manservant for the CEO of the production company, but we would be fulfilling yet another of my childhood dreams in the name of *Beast Hunter*.

After an uneventful flight from Boston to Vancouver followed by an easy cab ride, I arrived at our hotel about six hours before the Brits – the entire crew being from Bristol in England. For anyone who's never been to British Columbia – you should fix that as soon as possible. It is shockingly beautiful. Vancouver has been ranked one of the "most livable cities in the world" for over a decade, and at the time of writing has the third highest quality of living of any city on Earth. Downtown Vancouver reminds me of San Francisco's financial district with less hills and no fog, but when you get outside the downtown area into what would be urban sprawl in most other cities you encounter unparalleled natural beauty. Vancouver is, of course, a major port city on the Pacific, but unlike other port cities its harbors and waterways appear to range from "untouched" to "somehow enhanced by human occupation." This is a sharp contrast to the famous "dirty water" of Boston, the river fires of Cleveland, and the toxic shellfish of the greater NYC area. There are plush pine forests that, even from the back of a cab, make the air smell like a real-life glade plug in, and walkways along the water that appear to be straight out of a Cialis commercial.

I had decided to explore this little chunk of paradise while waiting for the crew to arrive, so I bought some delicious local beer and fish at a cool little outdoor joint near our hotel and proceeded to eat and drink contentedly while looking out on beautiful Horseshoe Bay. The air was fresh, the fish was fresh, the beer was fresh – beers, plural, I should say, I may have had a few. What I'm trying to say is – I drank alone for a couple of hours, but it was happy outdoor drinking. Vancouver sort of does that to you. While eating (drinking) I kept finding my gaze drawn to the top of this boulder-and-tree strewn hill on the edge of the water. There was a rocky outcrop at the peak that looked like the perfect place for a photo of the bay with my new DSLR, a "congratulations" gift to myself for actually getting a TV series after six-plus years of trying. Thoughts of the images I could now create of the sun tucking majestically behind the mountains, perfectly highlighting the quaint shops in mid-frame and causing bright flares in the foreground as it reflected off the water sharpened my resolve.

I had one more beer, paid my tab, and stood up. Actually, maybe that last beer wasn't the best idea of my life, but climbing that mountain before sunset clearly was. I started towards what had looked like a hill but was looking more and more like a mountain as I approached it. There were "no trespassing" signs at the base, no apparent trail, and a road with signs indicating that if you don't own a home on the mountain, you shouldn't *really* be on it. I found a couple of punk-rock kids milling around, looking disaffected, and asked about the veracity of these signs. They told me not to pay any attention to them and that "it was really sweet" at the top. That was all the encouragement I needed.

I started scrambling up the densely forested and deceptively steep slope. I had clearly misjudged the ease of this hike, and my sobriety. I stumbled a few times, and fell off one small ledge, landing in some pine needles and laughing like an idiot, found myself not so much hiking up the mountain as pulling myself up it. I was dramatically throwing my bag up onto boulders, then scrambling up myself, grabbing tree branches and hoisting my weight up, etc. It was not easy, and I was sweating a lot.

I love bouldering, Mt. Katahdin in Baxter State Park is one of my favorite climbs, and features nearly two miles of bouldering, but as a general rule I don't hike or climb while drunk. In fact, the most dangerous activity I participate in while drunk is karaoke. At the time, I thought my stupidity in this undertaking was pretty funny, but looking back on it – no one knew where I was, I was in a "no-trespassing" area where no one was likely to look for me, and I was not exactly on top of my game – it seems reckless to the point of idiocy. Basically, this was a perfect recipe for a scenario that ended with me chewing off one of my limbs in order to escape some self-inflicted fate.

After about an hour and a half I pulled myself up onto a rock and stood up, only to come face to face with two small blonde-haired and blue-eyed children playing ball in a well-manicured back yard. We froze and stared at each for a few seconds, and then they screamed. I had gotten off track – and given that there was no trail this shouldn't have been a surprise – and wandered into someone's backyard. Fearing being shot at or arrested and imprisoned for trespassing and scaring children, I quickly jumped down the little rise I had just come up on and ran, awkwardly. I looked up and saw a Mercedes maybe 10 yards away. I hadn't noticed, but for the previous 30-or-so minutes I had been hiking parallel to a very steep and windy road, and had entered a gorgeous and extremely wealthy suburban neighborhood.

I now followed the road up and down and up and down, occasionally moving aside for a Bugatti or a Bentley, whose driver would invariably wave to me – not yell obscenities, threaten to call the police, or stare in wide-eyed wonder at the dirty outsider, but wave and flash a friendly smile. It was clear I was not in Malibu – nor was I anywhere near that rocky outcrop I had seen from my comfy table in the sun at the base. Also, my sense of direction has never been great, and it turned out the sun would be setting at an angle that would prevent the previously imagined majestic photos, even if I could find a spot to take them. Added to this, I was very aware that I could, at any moment, inadvertently wander into someone's backyard again, or maybe the kids from the first yard had already called the Mounties on me. I'd reached about as close to the top of the mountain as I felt like I needed to, so decided to head back into the woods for cover – because that wouldn't make me look suspicious or creepy at all – and attempt the treacherous hike down in the growing darkness at a bit of a trot, as I was supposed to meet the crew in about half an hour. After nearly breaking my ankle twice in the first five minutes, I decided to return to the restricted road and deal with the Mounties if I had to.

I didn't see any Mounties, but I did see a lot of unbelievably nice Canadians. This was clearly high-value real estate. It was a neighborhood of which, had it been in America, I would have been kicked out, best-case scenario, probably by armed police or private security. I had no reason to be there, was very disheveled and sweaty, and a bit drunk – but none of the wealthy Vancouverites seemed to mind. They all waved to me, asked me how I was enjoying the evening, or commented on the gorgeous view. Families actually gathered in their backyards, arm-in-arm, to admire said view. It was a little *Stepford Wives*, but mostly really nice. I even saw the original kids I had scared, with their very attractive parents, playing outside. The kids waved to me and laughed. God, Canadians are awesome.

To this day I have no idea how I got to the part of the mountain where I ended up. When I finally reached its base, I was far away from where I started and had to hail a cab because I had no clue how to get back to the hotel – and Uber hadn't been invented yet. I arrived at about the same time as the crew, who had been conveniently delayed at the airport.

We all hugged, caught each other up on our lives since we had last hung out, and started what would turn out to be the most gluttonous shoot of the series. As a team, we were used to food shortages where you ate as much as you could and stocked up when you had a chance because it might be days before you got another opportunity for a good meal. If you operate under this mentality in a part of the world where food is not only everywhere but also hearty and delicious, you end up eating and drinking to capacity and having a car full of snacks and leftovers. Which we did. That first night was pizza and beers – again, all local, organic, craft, and delicious.

The next week was a blur of pure marine-bio joy. We were on the water every day, kayaking, boating, fishing, exploring tidepools, whale watching, feeding dolphins, etc. I was geeking out on the regular, exclaiming, "My first Sun-Star! I've always wanted to find one of these!" and "Check out these anemones! And Sea-Squirts! Sea-squirts are actually tunicates and some of our most ancient relatives! When they're young, they are free-swimming and have notochords, which are a pre-curser for spinal cords, kind of like amphioxus! One of my favorite professors, Dr. Burn, used to sing a song about amphioxus, want to hear it?" It was probably a little obnoxious, but everyone humored me. They could see how much I was enjoying it.

When the crew was filming cutaways, time lapses, and other beautiful shots that I wasn't in and ruining, I normally paid attention and tried to learn a little bit about the production side of filming, but on this shoot, I caught stuff. I caught snakes and lizards, fish and shrimp, urchins, crabs, worms, echinoderms of all shapes and sizes, and anything else I could grab. The entire shoot basically turned into a vacation for me, and the coolest part – the part I'd been waiting for and dreaming of – hadn't even happened yet.

I would be going down 1,000 feet underwater in a submersible. This was quite literally something I had been dreaming about and wishing for since I was five years old. For the purposes of the shoot, we'd be doing this to show "Caddy's world" – what the deep ocean is really like, and how mysterious and interesting it is, and to make the case for a huge creature hiding in the depths without humans knowing about it. Also, we wanted to show how quickly you can reach unbelievably deep water in British Columbia. We would be in a channel only a few hundred feet from shore, and the water would be between 1,000 and 2,000 feet deep! That's wild! This way, we could show just how close that "other world" is to habituated lands in BC.

As the day of the sub approached, I found it hard to think about anything else. This was a life goal that I honestly hadn't really expected to be able to achieve. It seemed like something James Cameron and Richard Branson would discuss over a meal of Swedish lobster in black truffles and ecologically sourced Densuke and Yubari melon wrapped in Bellota Iberico ham on one of their private islands.

"Richard, you must join me the next time I'm piloting a small submersible 1,000 feet underwater. It's simply the only way I can find true peace."

"Oh yes, James, I hear the Kermadek Trench is marvelous this time of the year."

Stupid rich guys in my head! It's marvelous all year, because it's one of the most stable and unchanging environments on Earth! Anyway, I was going to join this group of explorers, even if I was eating a steady diet of fried bar foods. It didn't matter, because I was going to be 1,000 feet underwater!

To say I was anxious the morning of the sub shoot would be like saying the Beatles were a pretty good band. Ben, the episode producer, picked up on my excitement and cruelly decided that I shouldn't be allowed to see the sub until the cameras were rolling, so I was left to wait behind a building while the sub crew prepped the equipment, and our TV crew got ready to film my reaction. I waited for four obscenely long hours. Playing on my phone, calling and waking up my wife, Anna, a couple of times, and finally resorting to the ultimate time killer for any young male – throwing rocks at an old cup. Every guy reading this knows this age-old game. Set up a target, any piece of trash, but preferably one that makes a satisfying noise when hit with a projectile, and throw rocks at it. Repeat until time is up. I had hit the cup at least 12 times (and I have horrible aim) when Ben finally popped his head around the corner and told me they were ready. The tension of the previous four hours absolutely melted away as I ran, grinning ear to ear, towards the dock. Anyone who has seen me run can attest to the fact that it is a sight which is embarrassing for everyone involved, like walking in on your parents showering together – no one involved wants to be there at the moment, no one is sure what is happening or what will happen next, there are possibly tears involved, and sometimes limbs move in haphazard and unexpected directions. My run was gloriously awkward, and then, all ideas of trying to look cool for the camera forgotten, I stared in schoolboy awe at the vehicle that would transport me to a new world – a world I had studied and dreamed about my entire life. My hand was shaking as I reached towards it in abject veneration, supplicating myself before the idol I had worshipped since boyhood. Not one, but two of the very few privately owned and operated homemade submersibles in existence stood before me, in all of their glory.

I'm told that the first time I went to the New England Aquarium when I was about five was an experience for my entire family. I do remember it, but all I can really recall is an overwhelming sense of awe and feeling like I had finally found what I was meant to do. Yes, at five years old, I came to the realization that the ocean needed to be a big part of my life. It was the closest thing to a religious experience I have ever had. My parents tell me that I walked in and stopped at the first tank, absolutely transfixed. I couldn't speak or move – I just stood there, glued to it, staring at the giant swirling, bright-colored fish. My parents let me stay about 10 minutes, then picked me up and moved me to the next tank. I had the same reaction. We slowly made our way up the perimeter of the aquarium, stopping at each tank for as long as my laughing parents and somewhat-amused-but-growing-bored sister could stand. At the top, at the octopus tank, I turned to them and stated in hushed, serious, tones that this was the greatest place on Earth, and I wanted to live here, or at least work here when I got older. And I did – I worked at the NEAq for about a year during college and loved every second of it. Once I set my mind to something, it's rare I let it slide without it happening, I just honestly believed until the day that I stood in front of the sub that this excursion under the sea was beyond my influence.

My parents are Al and Maribeth Spain, and in my opinion they are the best parents in the world. I could not possibly have had a better childhood, and that was in large part because of them. Mom said that the most important thing in the world to her was being a mom, and she excelled at it. She not only allowed me to be the weirdo adventure-nature-kid, she encouraged it. She saw my passions and nurtured them. She helped me to not be afraid to be who I am, and not let other people's hangups stop me from doing the things I love. Mom knows every kids' song, every kids' book, and every kids' activity ever created. She has one of each for every occasion, and generally a recipe for a special meal to go along with them. She made three meals a day (plus snacks) every day for my entire childhood. Even in college, I could walk in the house at 2 am and there would be a note on a plate of chicken parm saying, "heat for 2 minutes and enjoy. I love you." And I never once, not for a second, doubted that love. I always knew that, no matter what I did, how badly I messed up, she would always love and support me. Which left me free to take a lot of chances and risks, and really to become who I am, knowing that love was always there.

Al has always led by example, showing me how to be a good person, rather than telling me. Almost every minute I spend with him is a lesson on it. The quiet humility with which he would enjoy a street musician, giving the person $5 that we didn't have, but being so moved by the performance that he felt the guy deserved it for taking us out of ourselves for a few minutes while we watched and listened. Putting your family first, always. Never taking advantage of anyone for any reason – if you saw a weakness in someone, you'd help them, not exploit them. Money isn't the most important thing in the world – compassion is. Al both hits all of the "dad" tropes and breaks them as well.

First off, I call him Al, and always have. No one knows why. When I started talking, everyone would refer to him as Pop or Poppy – that's what my sister, Sarah, calls him – but I would laugh and just call him Al. Everyone tried to get me to call him anything else for a while but eventually gave up. All I would say in explanation was "that's his name," and, because my mom is SUCH a mom, the logic never failed. Her name might be Maribeth, but her real name is Mom. Even people who are not her kids call her Mom, and everyone calls Al, Al. It just works. So, yes, Al may have worn daisy-dukes to cut the lawn, and he likes war documentaries, and always, always, *always*, to this day, will ask "what route are you going to take" when you tell him you're driving somewhere far away – but he also plays every instrument and was in a soul band when he was 16 (technically too young to be in most of the bars they performed in), makes his own golf clubs, guitars, and other instruments, and would sneak me in to punk clubs when I was in 7th grade. He has a gold tooth, and Sarah and I got him his first tattoo for his fiftieth birthday. It's "MSPN" in the ESPN logo, and he got it at Fun City Tattoo on St. Marks in the East Village the day I introduced him and Sarah to Anna. MSPN is "Maribeth, Sarah, Patrick, Nathan" – Nathan being my genius brother who

15

is almost 13 years younger than me and comes into this story a bit later.

Also, and most pertinent here – my parents instilled a love of the ocean in my psyche, where it has become permanently lodged, and is almost a personality trait rather than an interest. We did not have much money growing up, but we saved enough every year to spend at least a few days at Seabrook Beach in NH. It was a paradise to us. Nothing else mattered while we were there. The place we stayed had no phone or TV, so we were completely cut off from the rest of the world and our normal lives. We were just there, as a family – playing cards, letting off fireworks, chasing down the ice-cream man, and being on the beach from the moment we finished breakfast to bedtime. Al and Mom would both talk about the infinite nature of the ocean – the endless vastness and the mysteries it contained. They'd get me books on its denizens and tide charts, and we'd have impromptu Earth science, biology, and physics lessons. Without getting too cheesy, the ocean became a metaphor for their love for me, and was the main driving force behind my going into marine biology.

Back in Vancouver I met John, the pilot of the sub, and immediately went into nerd overload, talking incessantly. Ben, I think more to get me to shut up than anything else, decided we should film some pieces to camera. That strategy didn't work, and I ranted and raved like a lunatic, and looking back at the footage now, I appear exactly how I felt – manic. Giving up on the idea of getting a coherent piece from me, I was allowed to explore and climb into the sub.

There were actually two subs – the first and smaller of the two was a one-man submersible that would accompany us on this epic journey in order to film our explorations. It was called Deep Worker, much to the delight of the incredibly immature James (sound recordist), Robin (our cameraman), and me. Deep Worker was sleek, black, and compact. It reminded me of a futuristic, fully-enclosed go-kart. It would have fit in on the roster of vehicle choices in *Mario Kart*. The viewing bubble was on top, which would mean the pilot would be sitting upright and looking over the top of the vehicle like a flying Jetson car. It had one large arm that split into two robotic "hands" on the front and was equipped with a multitude of lights and cameras.

The second sub, the one we would descend in, was called Aquarius. It was a more inviting white with an orange tower on top, orange tanks on the bottom, and a black-and-yellow salamander with the brand name Nuytco painted above the clear dome in the front – an expansive 180-degree viewing dome that would provide a view into my fantasy world. The sub was also kitted with all of the accoutrements of a good scientific underwater vehicle – lights, grasping arms, sucking tubes, specimen collection pods of all sizes, and enough hoses and gadgets to make it look like a prop in a Roland Emmerich film about exploring the moons of Saturn.

Before boarding, I peed for the eighth time, announcing to the crew (again) that I might pee my pants from sheer excitement when we hit 650 feet – the mesopelagic zone – then climbed in, still grinning like a crazy person. We had to film me getting into the sub five times because I kept messing it up. I would slip and swear, laugh, turn my back on the camera, or climb in without saying anything, face just plastered with that big grin, too excited to speak.

The first thing I noticed in the sub was how tiny the interior was. I would be lying on my stomach on a very short, thin, semi-cushioned plastic mattress similar to a camping pad with the greatest view in the world in front of me. The entire front of the Aquarius was a thick clear bubble, and my face was already pressed against it even though we hadn't left the ship. Ben climbed in and took his place on a camping pad to my right, and then John, decked out in fleece overalls (which apparently exist), climbed in to complete the trio of adventurers. He sat upright behind the two of us with our legs extending on either side of his fleeced lap. I imagine that it must have looked like some bizarre Christmas card — a dad sitting there with his two kids laying on their stomach at the foot of his chair, nestled in front of the fire while he reads stories to them, all of them grinning. The image of it still makes me laugh.

John was in his mid-forties, in good shape, and had salt-and-pepper hair. He had a deep, monotone voice with a pronounced Canadian accent. Everything about him screamed "scientist." He wore work boots, a lot of fleece, and an array of T-shirts that you get from various scientific conferences and projects, with slogans such as, "Intertidal Habitat Clean-up Day, 2005!" John was clearly as into engineering as I was into marine bio. We bonded immediately, swapping stories of past excursions, both in wide-eyed wonder at the others tales. He saw a six-gill *and* a thresher shark! I worked at an oyster hatchery. What kind of crustaceans had he seen on his dives? What kinds of filtration system did the hatchery use? *Of course* I want to hear about the eel you saw! Of course *I* want to hear about the fish where you were in charge of! He was my kind of people. We went back and forth until Ben politely asked us to please stop because he was getting less cool just listening to the conversation.

John ran through the safety check and confirmed the communication channels between us, Deep Worker and the boat were functioning. He ran through a variety of checks, turning knobs, pushing buttons, and flipping switches. The exterior of the sub came to life! Lights turned on and off, claws moved up and down, propellers whirred, and rudders shifted. This was actually going to happen. Then Ben and our crew did our checks – batteries, sound tests, lights... lights might be a problem. Filming in the interior of a sub with a huge clear bubble in front of me would be challenging from a lighting perspective. John pulled what looked like a bare light-bright board out of God-knows-where and stuck it in the tiny space between my mat and the viewing bubble. It illuminated me from underneath and Ben thought it had a nice, creepy effect. John said it had more than enough charge to last the duration of the trip. Ben was satisfied, I was about to pass out with heart palpitations, and John asked if we were ready as we heard hydraulic movement going on outside and felt the hook being fastened to the top of the Aquarius. Ben was also grinning now. We gave the thumbs up to the boat crew as the TV crew stepped into position. Ben hid under his omnipresent electric-blue compression-down bubble jacket, attempting to blend in with his mat and make it appear that only John and I were in the sub. Robin filmed as a crane lifted us, swung us overboard, and plopped us down in the frigid waters of the Agamemnon Trench in British Columbia.

The drop was a bit jarring and we hit the water with a little more force than I expected. Ben and I laughed nervously, but John seemed unfazed. We bobbed there for a few minutes as more switches were flipped and equipment buzzed. John checked with the boat, who gave us an "all clear to descend" as Deep Worker plopped, more gracefully than I expected, a few yards from us. I waved to the pilot (whose name I never found out). John pushed more buttons and pulled a few levers and we started sinking. As we slowly descended through the water column, I stared out of the front bubble and the oddest sensation crept over me. I was about to become one of less than 500 people in the world to head down to this depth in a vehicle like this, according to John. I was entering a virtually unexplored, pitch-black world filled with little known and even unknown creatures. This was it – the coolest thing I had ever done. Holy shit, it was actually happening!

The water in the first few feet was sea-green, then it quickly changed to a look of overcooked spinach, then a murky brown. The BC waters are brimming with life – such a multitude of small organisms that you can barely see through them, in fact. The visibility was pretty minimal for about the next 20 minutes, but I was completely enthralled by the thick cloud of cnidarians, ctenophores, copepods, and amphipods we were passing through, and was still talking a mile a minute to Ben, who nodded kindly every now and then to humor me. I began singing the Kenny Loggins classic "Danger Zone" to commemorate our passage into the next oceanic layer. When it happened, though, I was hushed into awed silence. We hit that magic depth, 650 feet down – the twilight zone. I couldn't even bring myself to hum the theme tune, however. I couldn't speak, truly and utterly dumbstruck.

There aren't words to describe the dark at the bottom of the ocean. It's not the same as a cloudy night in the middle of the Amazon, or even losing electricity in a room with no windows; it's more of a muted, free-falling-down-a-bottomless-hole darkness. Not an absence of light, but rather a feeling that light doesn't exist, like it's spread too thin for your eyes to notice, like light is not real, or only a memory. It's incredible, peaceful, calm, overwhelming, enveloping, and awesome in the truest sense of the word. I couldn't see the other two guys, but knew they must have the same expression on their faces as I did. Even John, who had done this dozens of times, said, "It never gets old. This part never stops amazing me or being exciting."

When he flipped the lights on in and outside the sub, sure enough we were all grinning open-mouthed like fools. "Wow" was just about all we could say. The world outside, caught in the halogen lights of the sub, was alien and surreal. It couldn't possibly be on Earth. How could this actually be on the same planet I'd lived on for 30 years? How could these animals, so foreign, so magnificent, so utterly "other," exist in the same world as the mundane surface existence I had led my entire life? This was a place like I'd never dreamed of and yet exactly what I'd hoped for. When a squid shot by and inked, I nearly cried. How could this squid live in a world with McDonald's in it? How could this landscape have existed the entire time I was shopping at Crossgates mall? How could I possibly go back to that world knowing this was here?

The squid ink was nothing like I had imagined – in all honesty, the entire landscape was nothing like I had imagined. The squid was tiny, only about four inches long, and its ink wasn't a cloud like in a Bugs Bunny cartoon, where a poof of ink would be shot into the face of its would-be attacker to shield its getaway. Instead, it was a much more practical and evolutionarily-believable wriggling blob. It looked like it had a membrane around it, but that was probably an osmolality-created illusion, I'm guessing surface tension. But either way, it appeared like a living, wriggling, little creature for about 30 seconds. It would certainly look like an easy meal to a predator, much easier to eat than the squid, and it was slower and moving in a different direction. A predator would likely make a quick decision and go after the easy meal only to get a mouthful of ink instead of a tasty squid, who would be far out of sight by the time they realized their mistake.

Watching the squid was like a repeat of my first trip to the aquarium – everything else in the world was completely shut off. As the squid swam out of sight, I became vaguely aware that we were still descending. I asked John how deep we were and after consulting a gauge, he told me we were at about 700 feet. He was communicating back and forth with the ship and Deep Worker using call signals. We were "AQ," Deep Worker was "Deep Worker," and the ship was "Topside." The voices on the radio sounded tinny, wavy, and somehow hollow.

"Deep Worker this is AQ, Deep Worker this is AQ, do you copy?"

"I copy AQ, this is Deep Worker, I have visual of you, I am dark."

"Deep Worker, this is AQ. Deep Worker you are clear to light up."

And light up it did. It was bizarre seeing this spaceship just appear in front of us, it looked so out of place in the world we had just started to explore. Ben began communicating, asking Deep Worker to get particular shots. We buzzed by each other a few times, Deep Worker "swimming" in circles around us. John seemed nervous – a collision at this depth, even a fender-bender, would be, in the immortal words of Egon Spengler, "bad," I wasn't thinking about any potential danger, though, and anything Deep Worker did was more of a distraction from my real focus – taking in everything I could and burning it into my memory. It seemed important that I try to remember every single detail. The interior of the sub was cool – not cold, but cool – and smelled a little stale. The mat was comfortable, and the world outside of the bubble was the most fantastic sight I had ever seen. I didn't know if the lights were more likely to draw animals in or repel them – John told me he found both to be true at different times.

I was vaguely aware that we were struggling to get some of the shots Ben wanted. Deep Worker was having some technical issues and one of our lights was out. John asked if we'd like to "touch bottom" – Ben and I giggled because we are super mature, then said a resounding "yes." The bottom had a thick – maybe two foot – layer of loose sediment. We disturbed it by touching down and lost all visuals for about five minutes until it cleared. We had landed in a field of inverts, mostly worms. I wondered how many of them were new species. We know so little about the deep oceans, especially the inverts down there. Nearly every expedition that wants to go through the paperwork can name a few new species if they bring a bucket of mud back up to the surface. We also saw a few small fry moving slowly with the grace and control that only a benthic species can muster.

We stayed on the bottom for as long as our schedule would permit, which was a little over four hours. We laughed, ate coconut M&Ms (which Ben had bought to prove a point about how disgusting American chocolate is, only to find that we both really enjoyed them, but maybe it was the location. I'd never eaten them before, or have done since), struggled to find the words to express what we were seeing, and just took it all in. At one point I felt water dripping onto my legs and thought dying down here wouldn't be the worst way to go. Ben must have felt the same thing because we both turned to face John at the same time. He was laughing and by the expressions on our faces knew what was happening. "Moisture from our breath and sweat will generally rise, hit the ceiling, condense, then drip down on us. Don't worry, if we'd sprung a leak, we'd know it before the water hit your legs."

This was reassuring, and Ben and I both played it cool, but until that moment I honestly hadn't even thought of the danger we were in. We were in a homemade submersible, privately owned and operated, with 441 pounds per square inch of pressure crushing us from all sides. I didn't get any feelings of claustrophobia, though – I was too busy just being in it.

Laura, our remarkable associate producer, called from what seemed like light years away, and her wavering hollow voice reminded us that if we didn't get back soon, we'd miss our ferry to the mainland, and hence our flight. Ben, because he knew this was a once-in-a-lifetime experience, radioed back to see if she could book a water taxi, as we needed more time. I've never been so grateful for an extra 30 minutes.

Laura, or Lady Laura of Clifton Wood as we called her, is, as seems to be a prerequisite for working at Icon, remarkable in every way. She adapted to any situation with ease – going from "one of the guys," to arguing with a porter who was ripping us off, to exhibiting the poise and grace of a royal, as her nickname implies. She definitely had the most geniality of everyone on the crew, but could be as raunchy as any of us and would often start a conversation with a put-on Cockney accent, "Oi, chappy, wha'we inta ta-dai China?" She taught me about rhyming slang. Somehow, China = plate, which rhymes with "mate," and mate means "buddy." I never got it. She immediately felt like a long-lost relative. Being a woman got her no special treatment from us (and she wouldn't have taken it if we'd tried), but being a very attractive young woman did get her a lot of special treatment from our guides, which we all benefited from. She's average height, just about my age, pale and freckly, with a devilish grin and piercing gray-blue eyes. She normally wears her long, curly, auburn hair pulled back in a ponytail. She has exceptionally good taste in music and often provided the soundtrack for long journeys – even Ben, a musician himself and opinionated gormandizer, was always happy to turn over control of the radio to Lady Laura.

Let's keep introducing folks, shall we? James, the sound recordist for every episode of *Beast Hunter*, is the most positive person I've ever met. He's five years younger than me, exceptionally handsome, blonde haired, blue eyed, scruffy bearded, incredibly bright, has been everywhere and seen everything, and is nearly always in a fantastic mood. Basically, everyone at Icon is amazing and some of the greatest, most talented people I've ever come across, but even among this group of superhumans, James is a standout. Not only is he talented in literally all aspects of production (he directs, produces, edits, writes, is a cameraman, sound recordist, drone operator, first responder, and general tech for all equipment), but he's an amazing guy and a great friend. He's hysterically funny – *very* inappropriate, but extremely respectful to every person he comes in contact with. He always asks for people's names and actually listens and pays attention to whomever he is speaking with. His partner, Jen, is just as kind, talented, and wonderful, and they have two amazing girls who will probably never know how lucky they are to have these two as their parents.

Your Grandmother would describe Ben as "devilishly handsome" and, with a smile and blush, tell you to "watch out with that one." He has a perpetual look of mischief about him.

Like any minute he might shout "Got you!" and something you'd taken for granted, like his name and age, would be revealed to have been incorrect. I wouldn't be at all surprised if the next time I see Ben, I find out he's actually a middle-aged Brazilian man named Jao – he would explain this in a thick Portuguese accent revealed to be his real voice. Ben (Jao) would remain a very close friend even after this revelation because Ben is incredible. There's also a slight chance that he is the elusive Bristolian street artist Banksy.

He's ageless – again, if it was revealed that he was in his 20s or his 40s I wouldn't be surprised either way. He has a runner's build and is an avid biker. His complexion is dark and swarthy but his eyes are light, almost a yellowish-tan ringed by a vibrant and captivating dark green. He's usually a bit scruffy and definitely looks the part of "explorer." You can tell before he opens his mouth that he has the best stories of anyone in the room, and you aren't wrong, he absolutely does.

Ben has been everywhere and done everything. I won't attempt to tell any of his stories here, but will say he's wrangled wild Komodo dragons and spent time in an Afghan prison after illegally breaking into an abandoned Soviet-era biological weapons facility for a documentary. Unlike many people in the exploring industry, Ben's stories aren't readily accessible and usually require a few drinks and some quiet pauses before they come to light, which makes them more exciting. Ben is not a guy who can't wait to share and attempt to one-up someone during a raucous conversation, although he easily could. He's a musician and a wonderful father to two incredible boys, one who looks like a mini-Ben, and a younger one who is perhaps double his brother's size, blonde, and displays the Irish complexion of Ben's incredible partner.

Ben frequently wears Ben Sherman and other hipster-chic brands in the jungles and forests, and avoids having his photo taken at all costs. Ben is extremely "cool," and I mean that in the best possible way. I think everyone who knows him admires him, and tries to emulate him in a way usually reserved for older brothers or your older sister's boyfriends.

Once, in Brazil, we were being eaten alive by insects, and were covered in mosquitos and bees. The bees were particularly nasty because they would give tiny annoying stings, causing you to swat them, and the resulting gory mess would stink like old fish and attract more bees. I offered Ben my spare insect-proof head covering – basically, a mesh bag that went over your head. Ben seemed delighted and grateful, then went to put it on, feigning a struggle to get it over his head. Grunting in exaggerated exhaustion and miming the inability to pull it over himself, he handed it back and said, "Sorry mate, I physically can't wear anything that lame. My body rejected it."

Ben works extremely hard at appearing to not work at all. He would stay awake hours after all of us planning out the next day's shots, then downplay the importance of each, saying, "I think it might look good if we X, but whatever you feel would be best, TV's Pat Spain," or "Right, so, the way I see it, if we do X, we won't need to work the rest of the day, yeah?" In fact, Ben never took time off. He was always working, and all of us wanted to please him. Every idea he had for a shot was brilliant, and the only hard part was reining him in, which was Laura's job, so the rest of us just enjoyed the ride that was being in Ben's company.

Ben normally seems nonplussed about everything. He takes it all in his stride. He doesn't sugarcoat things either, which I always appreciated. When I would flub a scene, Ben would say, "Right, that was shit. Do it again, but better, yeah?" with a huge smile. He generally has a big smirk and appears to just be taking everything in but not really being affected by it. To say he is unimpressed would be incorrect – he just seems *equally* impressed by everything. Like, we might all be admiring a gorgeous sunset over the Amazon river when Ben would walk over and join us after working on tweaks to a script, he might say, earnestly if a bit distracted, "Wow, pretty, yeah?" with a jutting bottom lip and a slightly impressed head nod. Then, after a pause, "All right, so what I'm thinking for tomorrow is..." You rarely got more praise than that. This was a side effect of having been everywhere and done everything. He had truly seen it all before and did appreciate it, but was not often moved in the way most humans are. So when, at the bottom of the ocean, Ben poked my side and I turned to face his massive open-mouthed grin, and he said in hushed tones, with eyebrows raised, "*This* is cool. *This*, TVs Pat Spain, is *cool*," while pointing out the dome, I knew I was truly experiencing something unique.

We wandered over a rock wall, descending still deeper, and touched down on a more sandy surface. The floor was covered in squat lobsters! The rock wall had inverts crawling all over it and fouling communities like I'd never seen. Tube worms, huge, gorgeous anemones, multiple barnacle species, etc. It was evident that we had barely scratched the surface of this new world. John told us he had spent a few nights down here because he'd been so entranced that he didn't want to surface, and saw something new on almost every dive.

On this trip, we hadn't seen anything that I couldn't at least identify its genus, and yet everything was remarkable. I could tell Ben was getting worried, however. We'd spent a lot of money on the sub and taken a big risk, and it looked like it would pay off as an experience, but not as a sequence for the show. As the sub lifted off the bottom, I saw what looked like a small Humboldt squid shoot past the window and ink. I was ruminating on what could have disturbed it – aside from the two giant spaceships, of course – when, out of the depths I saw one of the most amazing things I've ever seen. A mammoth lion's mane jellyfish was swimming along, trailing its meters of stinging tentacles, and suddenly it hit me. This was why we were down here – to see this monster in its natural habitat, where a 15-foot jellyfish makes sense. It's perfect, it's graceful, it's beautiful, and it's real and alive. On the surface, its tentacles would be stuck together, clinging to each other, the bell would be smushed looking, it's movements would seem jerky and ungainly. It would be odd and out of place, but down here, monsters make sense. Monsters are real. Monsters are undiscovered and lurking just outside of the lights of the sub. This is the unexplored world that every kid dreams about.

In that glorious lion's mane jellyfish, we had the shot we needed. We'd also had the experience of a lifetime. Ben had been ignoring Laura's increasingly frustrated calls to us to make us aware that we were *really* off schedule now. He would pretend we couldn't hear her, then grin at John and me: "A few more minutes I think, yeah?" We finally surfaced, were picked up by the ship, and climbed out of the sub, changed forever. A very nervous Lady Laura paced back and forth, looking at us reproachfully, seeing our budget skyrocket if we missed the next couple of boats and planes because of our decision to stay down there. Ben and I were apologetic, but couldn't stop smiling. We did our best to explain the experience to James and Robin while Laura sorted a water taxi. A man arrived a few minutes later and was paid a bit extra to exceed all reasonable speed limits and get us back to our car, where our kit was basically thrown into the back with little regard for the careful Tetris-like ritual normally reserved for the task, and James drove our sweet minivan like it was a nitro-powered hotrod. We listened to some Johnny Cash as Ben reflected that he was now one of two directors he knew of to have directed boat to boat, plane to plane, helicopter to helicopter, and sub to sub.

"The other one? Oh, a little-known director, more of an industry guy, less known to the mainstream. A man named James Cameron."

Even Laura was laughing by the time we made it to the next boat, with a couple of minutes to spare. Ben and I decided that, from that point on, we'd casually start any future travel story with: "So, when I was on the bottom of the ocean..."

## Chapter 2

# The Worst Game of Kabaddi Played in Cape Cod

The excursion 1,000 feet under the sea looked like it would be one of the most exciting moments of my life, but Canada, as a whole, was also one of the least exotic shoots in terms of destination. We would be filming all over Vancouver, Nanaimo, Cape Cod, Boston, Cambridge, and NYC, so Anna (my wife) and I would serve as fixers and translators for our British friends – helping to accustom them to our strange North American ways. We started in NYC, where we did the famous "stand still in Times Square and film a time-lapse of everyone moving around you" shot. I believe this is mandatory when filming there. Standing stock-still for nearly 30 minutes on a corner of Times Square tends to draw some attention. I was called an asshole for not responding to questions, invited to suck various body parts of angry pedestrians, slapped good-naturedly a few times by people who saw the cameras pointed at me, and kissed, once, by Anna.

We also needed a shot of me getting out of a cab. To accomplish this, I had to convince multiple cabbies to drive me about 300 yards. This was not as easy as you'd imagine. A typical conversation with a cabbie went something like this:

"Where you goin'?"

"See that group of people up there with the cameras? I just need you to drive me to them and let me get out of the car."

"No."

"I will pay you $10."

"Why?"

"They are filming me and need a shot of me getting out of the cab."

Here is where reactions differed – some would immediately

drive away, angrily. Others would appear absolutely terrified and ask me something along the lines of "Is this legal?" I would reply that I didn't see why it wouldn't be. Some cabbies would just leave, others would start shaking with terror, ask for the money up front, then, after dropping me, pull away looking shaken. One driver asked "Terrorist?" in a trembling voice. I assured him that I was not a terrorist, and then he asked for $15 upfront before agreeing to drive me.

The trip also provided yet another remarkable experience that I would never have had if not for the series. We received permission to film in the New York Public Library before it opened one morning. The library was massive in its emptiness. It's such an iconic location, and being there when it's completely empty was surreal. We filmed throughout the massive structure, but focused most of our efforts on the rare books, archives, and manuscripts room, which requires special permission to enter. It houses some of the most remarkable works of the Western world. I walked by a Guttenberg Bible, original notes from Darwin, and some manuscripts from my favorite authors as I approached the Charles Fort collection. This room contains all of the surviving notes of my great uncle Charles Fort, prophet of the unexplained and godfather of paranormal research. I was given the incredible opportunity to pour over his notes, reading his handwritten thoughts and ideas, as well as margin entries on various newspaper clippings which he had archived in some bizarre, seemingly random system. After a few hours I found what we'd been looking for – Fort's thoughts on sea monsters. It seems he took their existence for granted and said he wouldn't really do much research into them because "significant amounts of writing on the subject already exist" – and if it already existed, Fort wasn't interested.

Anna and I met in 1999 at Suffolk University in Boston, Massachusetts, when she was a freshman and I was a sophomore. I will never forget the first time I saw her, as it was the only time in my life I have been left literally speechless by a woman I've never spoken to. She was in a dress on her way out for the night, and I was in some dirty army pants and an old Ramones T-shirt hanging out in the cafeteria. I pretended to study the over-head menu for the entire duration she was in line and made awkward eye contact a few times, but was physically unable to speak. She was probably (rightfully) weirded out by me. She made her exit, I regained my ability to function, and I told my friends that the most attractive woman I'd ever seen had just walked out of the room.

I figured out who she was a few weeks later when it turned out that I'd be the Teaching Assistant in her intro to chem lab. I spent the next few years getting to know her – teaching a couple of her labs, assisting the teacher in others, hanging out occasionally as friends, selling her my old books. Any excuse to talk to her. I literally wrote things down to say to her the night before our labs together, then lost my nerve and just talked about the subject matter at hand, or her trip to Vietnam when she was 14 (my go-to "hey, I know a fact about you!" bullshit discussion). I sat awkwardly on my lab stool flicking my gloves against my thumb to make them "pop" and stared off into space, because I'm super cool like that. I finally got the courage to ask her out on a date at the start of my senior year. She had transferred to a different university in Boston and we were both single, and to my amazement she said yes. Our first date was at the New England Aquarium – which is the most Pat Spain thing to do, ever – and it was closed – which is actually *the* most Pat Spain thing to do, ever. We then went to a nice Italian restaurant, and when I tried being classy and asked if we should order some wine, she looked really nervous, and said, "Ummmm... I better not."

To which I replied: "Oh, I just thought wine might be nice. I'm not trying to get you drunk and take advantage of you or anything." Those words actually left my mouth.

She just said: "I mean, I'm only 20..." For those of you not in the States, the drinking age here is 21, and Anna was only trying to avoid an awkward situation of not being able to produce valid ID to get a drink, so of course, I created a *much* more awkward situation. She married me. I still don't know how or why.

Anna is 5'3" and fiercer and more loyal than anyone you could meet. She's first-generation Vietnamese and grew up in Lowell, Massachusetts, former Crack Capital of America, which, if she's been drinking, she will usually tell you in the form of a shouted "I'm from LOWELL" and an implied "Don't fuck with me or my family" – sometimes it's not "implied" so much as "implicitly stated." She's amazing in every way – an amazing mom, funny, kind, and supersmart (she destroyed me in organic and all other chem classes, overall grade point average, and, you know, life). She was working full time in the chem lab of the same biotech company I worked at (in the connected micro-lab) so didn't get to come on many shoots. She'd been an integral part of *Nature Calls*, the web-based series I did before *Beast Hunter*, and I missed being with her on location. She loves NYC and was happy to be part of the production. We left NYC after a delicious meal at Meatball and the procurement of some unusual souvenirs from Koreatown and headed back to our apartment in Winthrop, MA, just outside of Boston.

Upon arriving in Boston, I was determined to have the Brits walk the Freedom Trail, but because of time constraints contented myself with pointing out all of the places where our forefathers defeated theirs as we went by.

"Welcome to Faneuil Hall. This is where freedom-loving Americans plotted to overthrow your tyrannical, imperialist, rule. Now you can buy saltwater taffy, Matt Damon dolls, signs with the 'Rs' hilariously replaced by 'Hs' ('pahk the cah'), and overpriced hotdogs here. Because 'Murica."

"You're now standing on the spot where your monarchical ancestors shot an unarmed group of brave Bostonians for throwing snowballs at them, an event known as 'The Boston

Massacre,' which started the Glorious Revolution. Now you can buy 'Yankees Suck' T-shirts here."

James, a Welshman, feigned sympathy, saying his people had likewise been subjugated by the British dogs. Barny and Alex fought back, asking us how the colonies were fairing these days, and extolling the virtues of the crown. Boston finally had the last laugh when three bars refused to accept British passports as proof of age – something even I felt was a little beneath us. We eventually found an Irish bar in Inman Square that was happy to take any form of identification as proof of age, even a bar napkin which read, "Hear ye hear ye – to whom it may concern: the possessor of this scroll be at least 21 years of age. God save the Queen." Somehow, after a few beers, my mimicry of royal English began to sound like I was quoting Tolkien. We finished the tour of Boston with a classic New England seafood feast that, unfortunately, left big, tall Alex (our 6'10" associate producer and cameraman) running to the toilet all night. It seemed like suitable enough retribution, so I dropped the history tour the next day and just argued over the proper number of syllables in the word "aluminum," and the fact that a "car park" would be a place where cars would go to play with each other.

We were joined that morning by one of my best friends and the co-producer of *Nature Calls*, Dom, who would be taking publicity shots for the duration of the US shoot. We were to spend the day at the Harvard Museum of Comparative Zoology (HMCZ) and be treated to behind-the-scenes access to their impressive collection of preserved animals. They have ground-sloth skeletons and hides, bones of various gargantuan beasts from the Pliocene and other eras, a preserved coelacanth, a few thylacines, and enough oddities to make this the perfect setting for various *Beast Hunter* pieces. We were there close to dawn in an attempt to film as much as we could before the museum opened to the public.

Dom is one of my best friends. He's also one of the most

talented, driven, unique, and difficult to describe people I've ever met. He's an obscenely talented photographer, videographer, and sculptor who has won Best of Boston awards and been published in numerous international magazines, and much like Ben is always working and trying to make it seem like he isn't. It's a rare moment when Dom and I are not collaborating on, or at least planning, a project. It's what we both do – we absolutely love thinking up new ideas and making them happen. We live it, every day. It never feels like work when we are at a bar on a Friday night with our notebooks out planning our next adventure.

Dom is the consummate artist. I can't picture him not creating something or pushing himself towards the next goal. All of his varied living situations have been surreal walk-in art experiences. They've featured teepees, speakeasys, self-taxidermied animals, antiques, self-tanned animal hides, and, currently, a bed made from birch trees felled by beavers in his backyard and a fence stolen from my own backyard under the cover of night. In this, and many other ways, Dom literally lives art; but, because it is so engrained in his everyday life, he doesn't realize how remarkable his work is. To him, it's just his life. Like all great artists, he's never satisfied and never finished, which can be tough on those around him who want to see him happy. This sounds wrong – he *is* happy. He's one of the few people I know who really enjoys life, but he's rarely proud of any of the amazing work he's produced, and even the most outrageous and impressive things he does quickly fade into the background, replaced by the next once-in-a-lifetime experience or trip that, for nearly everyone else in the world, would be their defining moment – brought up at dinner parties, in college essays, or in their obituaries.

Trying to describe him is challenging. Do I describe Dom as he is today, the thoughtful, self-aware father who would rather spend a week in the woods with his amazing wife and son than a week documenting the orgies and bacchanalia that is Bonaroo?

Or do I describe the Dom of his early twenties, when he was living and breathing chaos? A man whose twenty-second birthday ended with a literal flood of beer, despite not having a drop himself (honestly, beer two inches deep covering the floor of a Mission Hill apartment) and a naked pudding wrestling session between himself and four female classmates in the kitchen? A man who would walk into Walmart to buy some bacon and end up playing a rousing game of soccer in the aisles, then pretend to fall and smash two dozen eggs on his way down, *years* before it was a YouTube meme? No, it seems wrong and unfair to describe him as such, partially because his thirties self would laugh and shake his head at the person he was if they met today, but mostly because that was only ever one small part of Dom – it was just such a loud, absurd, amazing, and engrossing part that it was all most people saw. Like a moth to a flame, everyone who saw this aspect of Dom's nature was drawn to him. Everyone was waiting to see what would happen next, and Dom *never* disappointed, and still doesn't. It would be inaccurate to say it was an act, or performance art – it absolutely was not. It was definitely Dom being himself, but it wasn't as 24/7 as you might think after only hanging out with him for a short time during one of these impromptu excursions. It also wasn't for anyone other *than* himself and his own amusement, which was also hard to see at first. It was easy to mistake as an act, a put on, for a rapt audience. But the more time you spent with Dom, the more you realized he would be doing this whether you were there or not.

I consider myself extremely fortunate to know the other side of Dom – the one *behind* the hedonistic Dom, even in those early days. I think few people can say this. Dom has a huge group of friends, many of whom have also become my close friends, but in the group, I think there are a select few of us, a sort of inner circle, who have gotten to know him as a whole person, and all of our lives are richer for it. The "Dom" I've been describing disappeared for all intents and purposes after one of his bike trips across the country, from which he returned a new man. With no planning or preparation, he pedaled a bicycle coast to coast, twice. After the first one, he came back calmer, more Zen-like in everyday life, saving the partying for appropriate times and then unleashing his inner Jell-O-wrestler when he was most needed. He also contracted scurvy as a result of his incredibly poor diet on the trip, and maybe getting a pirate disease which is literally cured with orange juice made him realize that he needed a slight lifestyle change. Probably not, though – I've never known Dom to change based on anything other than his own whims. After the bike trip, and the subsequent scurvy, Dom seemed able to channel his energy into being more productive and focused, taking on fewer projects and focusing entirely on photography, *Nature Calls*, and sculpture.

All of this aside, the main reason Dom was on this shoot was because of his talent as a photographer, his kindness, and his generosity. Dom's time is the most valuable thing to him, and is one of the things he is generous with. He budgets his time the way most people do their finances, and only spends it doing the things which are most important to him. He may not remember birthdays or Christmas, but Dom is always there for his friends when they need him. Whether it's tearing down an old shed, painting a couple of rooms, building a treehouse for your kids, or spending two days looking for a loose alligator in Rhode Island, Dom will be there. You can also count on him to make you amazing handmade gifts and postcards – sometimes showing up to family functions with ducks he just shot, maple syrup he spent a week collecting and boiling, or museum-quality framed photos that he's cut and mounted himself.

I suggested the HMCZ spot having spent a fair amount of time doing research there while attending Suffolk University. A marine bio class I'd taken had even involved a few days sorting through the museum's impressive collection of deep-water vertebrates. It was a bio-nerd's heaven. The entomology collection alone is worth a day, but we were rushing around as usual and barely scratched the surface of the impressive collections contained in those brick walls. The highlight for me was being able to hold the holotype skull of a forest gorilla. This was the skull used to describe the species, the exact skull that was sent to the Western world to prove the existence of a hairy man-like beast lurking in the forests of Africa. I was shaking as I picked it up, terrified that I'd drop or otherwise damage this important piece of history.

After the museum we were going to film "Pat Spain's daily life" at my day job in the microbiology labs – which was actually a night job as I worked second shift. I spent a lot of time at work in those days, a lot of time. My record was 21 days in a row with no days off and none of those work-days were less than 10 hours. Taking a few months off to film was an incredible and unexpected gesture from my team and boss. I knew what the extra workload would do to them and will be forever indebted for the opportunity. In addition to the time off, I was shocked and supremely grateful to get permission to film in labs and manufacturing space. The crew would not be allowed to enter the tightly controlled areas, but would be able to film from the viewing platform as I walked around in my head-to-toe particle-controlling and contamination-reducing gown (called a bunnysuit by all who work in the field), pretending to work. I had a plastic clipboard with blue, non-particle shedding paper, and walked from buffer tank to media vessel pretending to read various gauges and controls. The room was actually shut down at the time and the tanks were empty – a happy coincidence, and the most likely reason for our permission to film. In the labs, we mocked up some of the more impressive looking tests. In the sterility suite (where I spent most of my working days – up to 19 hours a day – testing finished pharmaceutical products for microbial contamination), I entered my spacesuit, in a plastic bubble, in a pressurized, tightly controlled room, and mixed some colored liquids together – because mixing colored liquids equals science. I also mocked up a chemistry assay (although I hadn't worked in chemistry for over six years at the time), which involved a facemask and flames – because fire also equals science. The shoot was really fun, and it was bizarre having my Icon friends and biotech friends together in one place. Worlds were colliding, and I liked it.

I love seeing depictions of science on TV. They nearly always show a scientist balancing a pH meter – not actually doing a test, just calibrating the instrument used for a very basic test, because it involves a red, a blue, and a yellow liquid. They are also often shown pipetting a pH buffer from one tube to another. These are generally unbelievably smart PhDs who do incredibly important work and probably hadn't calibrated their own pH meter in the decade before filming, but their real work doesn't involve fire or colored liquids, so TV magic. Another favorite is putting anything in or removing it from dry ice. As a bat researcher Dom and I once filmed said, while putting samples into the deep freeze: "When there's smoke and no fire, that's science."

So, we manufactured science for the cameras for a day then headed to Anna's and my apartment to get ready for a trip to the Cape that night. Barny (series producer) and Alex were tagging out, with Ben, Laura, and Robin stepping into their places. The whole crew chased our insane pug, Sushi, around our place while noshing on an incredible cheese plate Anna had prepared for us. Laura, once again our fearless assistant producer, made a run to buy supplies, which included a very large dead fish.

The next day we would be filming at the Woods Hole Oceanographic Institute (WHOI) to interview a few marine scientists, film some frozen samples in the famous Ketten labs -20°C freezer, and perform the first ever CT scan of a preserved oarfish, the largest bony fish in the world. The dead fish Laura picked up (a 21-pound bluefish) was to go in the freezer while a time-lapse camera focused on one of its staring dead eyes would capture the transition from "recently dead" to "frozen like a white walker." We all agreed this would make a really cool cutaway shot. Cutaways are basically filler shots used in transitioning from one scene to another – cars driving by in or out of focus, lights on buildings blinking, spiders building webs – all classic cutaways. A fish's eye freezing would be a stand-out one in an episode about sea serpents. While procuring said fish, Laura also picked up about five pounds of dry ice to produce a cinematic fog billowing out as the freezer door slid open. This would be yet another logistically difficult and time-consuming shot which, over a few drinks, we all determined would be "really cool" and "totally worth it." Science. Both shots were Ben's ideas, and both capture his absurd genius.

The ride down was uneventful. Despite being a marine biologist living in New England, I had never actually been to Woods Hole and was pretty excited to see it, but bummed to have to leave Anna back in Winthrop once again. WHOI is the preeminent marine research facility in the world with a pedigree boasting the discovery of the Titanic and the little-known and completely bizarre ecosystem of hydrothermal vents. Every marine biologist wants to work there, including me. I had been passed over twice when applying for internships, but now I had the last laugh! I was on TV – searching for a sea monster... yeah, it made sense that they passed.

Joking aside, Woods Hole recognized the value that shows like *Beast Hunter* bring to their profession. Big sexy discoveries like hydrothermal vents absolutely inspire the public and bring attention to important marine issues, which brings in much needed funding, but they are few and far between. Most papers coming out of a facility like WHOI deal with far less exciting issues such as population assessments of zooplankton or commercial fishing stock studies that usually reduce the allowable catch, thereby pissing off all fisherman and raising prices, not exactly endearing the organization to the public or capturing a childlike sense of wonder. Some "fun" science talking about a sea serpent is great PR and can inspire people (like it inspired me) to study other fascinating aspects of the marine environment. When we mentioned scanning an oarfish they jumped at the opportunity.

We arrived at our hotel pretty late and turned in so we could get a few hours' sleep in order to leave for WHOI before most of the vacationing tourists woke and clogged the single-lane roads. We arrived early the next morning bearing bagels, donuts, and coffee for everyone at the labs, a gesture that, as a former research marine biologist myself, I knew would immediately endear the crew to the scientists, and buy us a little leeway when we inevitably did something stupid, ran over our scheduled time, or made some other *faux pas* that goes with the territory of being a film crew but appears as rudeness to those who aren't familiar with the bizarre world of TV production.

Dom, Ben, and I received an all-access tour of the labs from a few top scientists while Laura and Robin setup for the shoot. Five minutes into the tour left me regretting every life decision that had pulled me away from marine-biology research. The place's reputation as the Mecca of marine science was clearly well deserved. I loved how unabashedly into their jobs everyone was, and they talked enthusiastically about them. Their work stations were decorated with *Far Side* cartoons and toys of whatever species they were focused on, and no one seemed to mind being at work. In fact, none of them treated it like work, and spoke about their research the way a comic-book collector talks about *Action Comics* #7, throughout which Superman inexplicably wears yellow boots. It was remarkable and entirely depressing as I would be going back to my day job when filming was done, and I liked my day job – but my God did I miss marine biology.

We arrived back at the labs just as Laura and Robin were finishing up. Robin is a very small, very British man with a very thick accent – Anna says she could only pick up about every fifth word from him, which is unfortunate, because he's hysterical. He was cameraman for a bunch of *Man vs Wild* episodes and won an Emmy for some famous, multiyear, huge-budget wildlife documentaries for various networks and, due to his height, was able to get some truly stunning shots – some of the best in the productions, if you ask me. His shots often look like someone is holding the camera down around their waist and shooting upwards, but miraculously maintaining perfect framing and focus. Well, he's not holding the camera down, it's resting on his broad but low-to-the-ground shoulders as he squats or kneels in painful-looking stress positions. He's scruffy and bespectacled, ruggedly handsome, muscular, and generally wears a fisherman's knit sweater and hipster cuffed, dark jeans.

Robin greeted us with something that sounded like "fish ear."

"Pardon?"

"Fish ear, whilyer gone, fish gah'ear."

Ah, the fish had arrived, good. He meant the preserved oarfish, the largest bony fish in the world. They can reach lengths of 30 feet (unconfirmed measurements put them closer to 40 feet) but are rarely ever seen, alive or dead. They are believed to be found in all the world's oceans, but, as an inhabitant of the open sea, your chances of bumping into one are slim. They are thought to eat tiny plankton as they move slowly in the water column, all 30 feet of them upright with their head towards the surface and their tiny, shimmering, red fins propelling them forward. They only come to the surface or to shore when they are dying, at which point their body flashes bizarre multicolored patterns (much like a dorado) as they undulate unnaturally in their death throes, looking distinctly serpentine. These facts have led scientists to theorize that many "sea serpent" sightings can be attributed to these bizarre creatures. We were to be the first people to ever perform a CT scan on one of them.

The CT scan would be a noninvasive way to essentially dissect the fish and answer some questions about its anatomy

– particularly its musculature – and give us insight into things like what it had eaten just before it died. In some ways, it was better than a dissection because there was no degradation of the specimen – no cutting away of an important clue without realizing it. We hoped to scan it for a few reasons:

1 – no one had ever done it before, and that would be very cool;

2 – oarfish are commonly cited as a "mistaken identity" for sea serpents – there was almost zero chance of finding a live one, so, the dead specimen was the best option to introduce it into the episode, and this scan would be more dynamic and exciting than just seeing it in a giant jar; and

3 – it was a great way to establish Woods Hole as a place where cutting-edge science takes place, and a way for me to geek out a bit more and show off my (marine) bio chops.

Our oarfish was a juvenile, around 12 feet long, which had washed up on a beach in Florida a couple of years before. We contacted the museum that had it, then contacted Woods Hole who had the CT scan, offered to pay to get the fish to WHOI, and magic followed. Everyone was excited to see what the scan would reveal about this little-known giant. The folks from WHOI prepared the CT machine while the fish's owner removed the pickled specimen from its massive container. It smelled strongly of preserving fluid and looked like it belonged in a huge jar on Professor Snape's shelf with its monstrous glassy eyes, pale brown flesh, and oddly shaped upturned mouth. The most impressive features of the oarfish (aside from its size) are its bizarre fins, which resemble more a bird of paradise's plumage than a pelagic fish's fins. It has bright red fronds sprouting from various spots and a crown-like plume on top of its head. In this case their color had faded from preservation, and they certainly didn't look as majestic as on a live specimen, but they did look weird. We laid it out on surgical pads and got ready to scan.

Ben asked me to get very close to the fish as Robin filmed

from different angles, climbing on chairs, lab benches, and under various pieces of equipment. He filmed me and the fish through the tubular opening of the CT scan and the fish from my perspective. The entire time, my face was inches from the face of this creature, sometimes looking at it, other times looking at the camera. We did about 45 minutes of this before I started giggling.

"What's wrong?" asked Ben.

"Nothing, sorry," I replied, shaking my head slowly and snickering.

"Why are you laughing?"

"I dunno… it's pretty weird looking, huh?"

"Um, yeah?"

"I mean, look at its face – blub, blub, blub. I bet that's what its mouth does – blub, blub."

"Pat, what are you doing?"

I was just about to "boop" its mouth when—

"I feel kinda weird. Kinda dizzy."

Just then, the guy from the museum walked in eating some chicken, which I found way too funny. He removed a drumstick from his mouth and asked, "How long has he been there, leaning over the fish like that?" "Probably about an hour, why?" asked Laura.

"He's drunk," he said casually, as he licked his fingers. "He's been breathing in ethanol for an hour. I preserved the fish in ethanol to make it easier to travel with."

"What?" asked Laura and Ben.

I started laughing again, and blurted in a singsong voice, "Yup, drunk, that makes sense. Blub, blub, blub. You're weird, fish. I like you, but you're weird."

Ben called a break to allow me to sober up. An hour later, we had eaten lunch and I had a pounding headache but was ready to film. I kept my distance from the alcohol-soaked monster this time. The scan revealed some remarkable things about the fish's anatomy, diet, and locomotion, like the variety and prevalence of other bony fish in its gut, and some fin-musculature that had never been documented. The fish was one of those incredible examples of "the more answers we get, the more questions we have," and remains a mysterious sea monster as I write this. The scientists at WHOI told us that at least five dissertations would come out of studying the results of our scans. They thanked us profusely for giving them the opportunity to do this, and we told them we were just glad it had worked out. It felt really good to be adding to actual scientific knowledge again. I missed studying oysters and estuarine fish, and being part of the scientific community. Here we were, making a TV show about cryptozoology and something we had done was going to lead to multiple dissertations. And I was able to get drunk in the process. It was a good day.

Next on the agenda was the deep freeze. We would be filming an interview with a world-renowned Marine Biologist in a -20°C walk-in freezer. This required us to don Antarctic temperature-rated thermal suits and other drool-inducing performance outerwear. We conducted the interview, released the biologist back into the wild, and started filming cutaways, introductions, and other "cool" shots in this bizarre room. The cooler was filled with hundreds of dead and frozen animals and animal parts, including a lion's head, about a dozen dolphins, a few giant sea turtles, a narwhal's head, a hippo, some gigantic squid beaks, and a 20-plus foot anaconda. These were all hanging from ropes and hooks, piled on shelves, and stacked in and on Home Depot five-gallon buckets. It smelled like a walk-in cooler at a liquor store rather than the cold storage on a fishing boat as I'd expected. It was also exceptionally dry, and it was this that actually bothered me more than the cold. I've spent time in -20°C walk-ins at work before, and I've also been in -40° and even -80° ones – but only for short amounts of time – picking up or dropping off samples. Spending real time – a few hours total – in one was not at all the same. With the explorer suit, boots, hat and gloves, you really only felt the cold on your face, and with no wind it wasn't terrible. But my lips chapped after about 10 minutes, and cracked after 45. My contacts felt like they were freezing to my eyeballs after about an hour, and the scientists recommended we limit our time to about 15-minute intervals after that.

After an hour of filming frozen dead things, we decided it was time for the bluefish. Robin, Dom, and James began rigging up a time-lapse close-up while Ben, Laura, and I went to the parking lot to collect the cooler. We joked about the importance of our job compared to those of the scientists as we walked back. Laura summed it up best: "I mean, it's pretty cool and all to win a Nobel Prize for the work you're doing on jellyfish cells and their application in oncology, but *we're* about to film a dead fish's eye for an hour."

We set the fish up for the shot, positioning it exactly right, getting lighting correct, etc., before realizing that Robin's camera wasn't working. It appeared to have frozen. After about an hour of James, Dom, and Robin disassembling, cleaning, drying, wiping, flicking, and brushing various parts of the very expensive piece of kit, we came to the unfortunate conclusion that it just didn't like being at -20, then nearly 90 (the ambient temperature outside and in the space between the labs and freezer), then back to -20, and so on, each time we left the freezer for a break, for more equipment, to swap out a lens, or to get something out of the car. We finally got it working at room temperature and decided the fish-eye shot, while cool, would probably take too long, might not work, and might damage the camera beyond repair. We also realized that, in our rush to help with the camera, Ben, Laura, and I had moved the fish with a lot of our other gear, and left it outside in the sun for an hour wrapped in newspaper on a 90-degree day. A bluefish does not smell great under the best of conditions, and we were not going to subject the nice folks at

WHOI to the lingering scent of 20 pounds of rotting percimorphi so we could *maybe* get a shot that had only a slim chance of being used in the finished cut.

We decided to instead focus on the "dry ice smoke as the freezer doors open" shot. For this, we had a few buckets, a lot of dry ice, and some water. Health and safety had warned us not to be in an enclosed space with large amounts of dry ice, and not to allow it to touch our bare skin – so of course we did both. We had contests to see who could hold it the longest (Laura won). I showed everyone how to make dry-ice bombs using plastic micro-centrifuge containers, a skill I learned from night shifts in the labs. My friend would make them and casually leave them near your chair or on the tabletop where you were working, walk away, and wait for them to explode a few seconds later, invariably causing you to drop whatever you were working on.

After a few well-timed bombs, we placed James in the freezer with two buckets of dry ice, some water, a mini-fan, and a walkie-talkie. He was instructed to radio us and let us know when enough "smoke" had built up to look impressive, but not enough to cause him to pass out. We must have tried this shot 45 times. We filmed it from different angles, using one bucket, then two, then four, holding the buckets in the air, Dom and James both inside the freezer, Robin in the freezer, dry-ice inside and out – and, after a while, we kind of got it, but not really. Ben would have kept going, but during a take when four of us were in the freezer we suddenly heard the sound of water *gushing* overhead. We froze, and then a bunch of alarms started sounding. We saw water pouring down one of the walls of the walk-in.

Scientists came rushing out to see what the commotion was as we stood there with matching hangdog expressions while Laura, our dedicated spokesperson, said, "I'm terribly sorry, but I fear we've broken something in there," in her best posh accent. We hadn't, we'd just overloaded the humidity and temperature controls – six of us in the cooler exhaling warm moist air for hours combined with the dozens of door openings and closings had let in far too much moisture and warm air, which had been building and building until something gave, which I believe was a pipe somewhere – okay, I guess that *is* breaking something. We apologized profusely to very understanding scientists and maintenance techs, who began feverishly working to contain the flowing water and fix whatever had gone on the fritz with the HVAC. We determined that this was our cue. Bagels and muffins only go so far towards buying friendships, and we once again apologized, thanked everyone for a lovely day, and hurried out of there. After getting in our rental van, we realized we'd left the fish behind. Once again, Laura shouldered the task with little more comment than "you guys suck," jumping out and tossing the stinking beast back in the cooler with the rest of the dry ice, gagging.

We got back to our hotel and decided we deserved a nice night out. Dom suggested a restaurant on the beach and, after showers and changes of clothes, we looked like a fairly respectable group as we entered a fine, upscale, Cape Cod establishment. Dining with a natural-history film crew is an experience – we tend to be a little loud, but not obnoxious; a little drunk, but not stumbling; and have very, very bizarre conversations. That night was no exception. After an amazing New England feast, and conversation running the gambit from "weirdest thing you've ever eaten" (kitten) to "how to make a tribe ignore the cameras" (Robin had the best anecdote for this one– a well-endowed female assistant producer he was filming with in Central Africa volunteered to go topless for the duration of the shoot. Apparently, it put everyone in the tribe at ease), we hit a bar across the street.

As a rule, Laura does not drink on any shoot until we wrap filming, but we persuaded her to have one beer with us. We were in very good spirits as we ordered pitchers of local beer and bartender-recommended mixed drinks. After very little business talk (shots we still needed to get, call times for the morning, car plans for next leg of the trip, etc), we moved on to one of our favorite topics — American culture vs British culture. After re-hashing some old favorites (pudding is a dessert, it is not *all* desserts), we moved onto sports. You would be hard pressed to find two Americans less qualified to talk about this subject than Dom and me. Despite living in Boston since 1998, I've mistakenly called a certain quarterback Tim Brady on more than one occasion and Dom is almost as ignorant. We tried to defend soccer (futbol) and American Football (football), and convince the Brits that a cricket is an insect, but only half heartedly. Eventually, this led to talk of extreme sports and Ben asked if we were familiar with Kabaddi. Unsurprisingly, we were not.

Kabaddi is a professional sport which, when described to someone, sounds like your kid brother invented it on a particularly boring rainy day. It's sort of a mix of wrestling, tag, and jailbreak with a key bizarre rule – you have to hold your breath during gameplay. To prove you are holding your breath, you must chant "kabaddikabaddikabaddikabaddi" in a mantra-like incantation for the duration of your "turn." Getting tackled, dragged to a different side, tagged, stepping out of bounds, or "held until you stop chanting" all cause you to be "out." Did I mention this is a professional sport? It's nearly as popular as cricket in India, Pakistan, and other Asian nations, and there is even a kabaddi world cup! The professional version involves a rough game of tag between very large, oiled-up, nearly naked men tackling and wrestling each other. The actual rules are incredibly hard to follow and complex, but the basics are as follows.

There are two equal numbered teams in an evenly divided two-sided court. You must stay within the lines or you are out. Each team has their own side of the court. One person from a team, dubbed a raider, crosses over to the other team's side. Here is where the breath-holding comes in – the raider must start chanting "Kabaddikabaddi..." as he crosses into the opposing team's territory. His goal is to tag an opposing player and run back to his own side before he runs out of breath. The other team's goal is to prevent this from happening. If he succeeds in making it back to his own side before running out of breath, the player(s) he tagged are out. Only one player can cross at a time, and teams take turns – one raider goes, then a raider from the other team, etc. So, the raider crosses, chanting "kabaddi" under his breath but loud enough to be audible to the other team and the refs, tags an opponent and tries to run back to his side, while an opponent grabs him and tries to hold him until he runs out of breath, and here the raider has another option – he can wrestle the person he just tagged! Yes, it is as awesome as it sounds, and no I am not making any of this up. While chanting "kabaddi," he can turn to his opponent and wrestle them to the ground – whoever hits the ground first or goes out of bounds is out, or, if he stops chanting during the wrestling, he is out. Each "out" is a point for the other team. I am unsure if you tally up the points at the end of a time limit, play until one side reaches a certain point total, or there's a quidditch-like game ender that I don't know about. We played "last-man standing" rules, which Ben seemed to think was acceptable. I HIGHLY recommend you start playing this game immediately. Start an intermural league, because it's the greatest sport of all time.

We were amazed. Much drunken googling confirmed the existence and popularity of kabaddi. Despite barely knowing anything about any sport, Dom and I instantly became fans. We needed to play, right away. As the bar was on the beach, we decided the sand would cushion our falls and set out to play our first, and possibly last, game of kabaddi. We drew a rough court in the sand, divided into somewhat equal teams, and started the greatest coed beach sport ever.

Robin was low to the ground and nearly immovable. After a particular good tackle on James, he ripped off his shirt and ran around his side in celebration, unfortunately crossing the line and thus removing himself from the game. Laura body-slammed Dom, which led to massive amounts of hooting and hollering from the rest of us. I wrestled a surprisingly competative Laura until she ran out of air but received a kick to the shin for my trouble. James was thrown violently by Ben and nearly broke an ankle. After I tagged Ben he grabbed my ankle, causing me to fall which knocked the breath out of me, and I was out. Ben was the kabaddi champ of the beach. We played a few rounds and ended up with some head wounds, bleeding limbs, and various twisted and bent joints, but it was worth it. Laughing, we got back in the van as Lady Laura, our designated driver, drove us to the hotel.

We fell out of the van nursing our kabaddi injuries but not ready to sleep. Despite the hotel pool clearly being marked closed, someone, probably Dom, suggested a midnight swim. Ben's pants were off before the word "swim" was fully uttered. To this day I don't know why, but he had a speedo on under his Ben Shermans, which was lucky for us and seemed to pleasantly surprise him. He hopped the fence and, laughing, Dom, James, Robin, and I followed (after grabbing our bathing suits). Laura was content to watch and laugh at us fools. We swam and joked for a few minutes until Ben got a dangerous looking gleam in his eyes.

"Robin, how long would it take to assemble the camera?"

"Five minutes, I reckon."

"Laura, do we still have that dry ice? Pat, what are your thoughts on nudity?"

"We do have the dry ice, but I don't think it should go anywhere near a nude Pat," said Laura.

I confirmed this. "I am fine with nudity on camera, but not my own."

"What if it was very tastefully filmed and I promise there will be no clear shots of your genitalia *or* nude bum?"

"Go on…"

I suddenly realized how "Girls Gone Wild" works, and how

easy it was to be talked into something like this. Ben's maniacal plan was not "Pat Gone Wild" – he was still upset about not getting the fish-eye shot, and thought we could make up for it by making a homage to *Apocalypse Now* in our hotel pool. He would put the dry ice in the pool and, as it bubbled and smoked, get a close-up shot of me emerging from the water like Willard – just the top of my head at first, then my eyes and slowly the rest of my face, staring into the distance. All of us loved the idea. Laura, being far and away the most reasonable,

"Where will we use this shot? It has nothing to do with anything else that we've filmed."

"It'll just be really cool. I know we can find a home for it."

"Why does Pat have to be naked if you're only filming his head?"

"I want him to *know* he's naked. The audience doesn't need to know, but it'll help if he does."

This last bit didn't make sense to any of us, so it was agreed that we would do the shot, but I would keep my bathing suit on. We tested it with a couple of small pieces of dry ice. Even a little one produced a surprising amount of smoke. Once we had that proof of concept, Ben tossed a big chunk into the center of the deep end and yelled "Action!" as he dove in after the ice, and the owner of the hotel walked out onto the patio saying, "What the *hell* is going on out here?"

We scattered like high-schoolers caught drinking in a cemetery. James and Robin were the first over the fence, giggling, and ran dripping into Robin's room and locked the door. We saw their laughing faces peering out of cracks in the blinds a second later. Dom and I were next, running a diversion by going behind the hotel, then circling back to our rooms in case we were being followed. Ben was last as he was underwater when the owner had come out. While running, then through our window blinds, we saw him pop up, looking confused about where everyone was, then notice the enraged owner. She was a very nice middle-aged woman who had been friendly to us earlier in the day. All traces of good humor were gone now as she stared at Ben and her smoke-filled pool.

Ben attempted an interesting conflict-aversion strategy – namely, pretending that he didn't understand a word she was saying and tried to play like everything was totally fine.

"I said, what the *hell* are you doing?"

"Swimming!" a grinning Ben responded while climbing out of the water, as if it was the most normal thing in the world, and proceeded to quickly gather his belongings and head to his room.

"Didn't you see the sign about the pool being closed?"

Ben pretended to not hear this. "Come again?"

"What's your name?"

"I'm sorry, what?"

"If you're staying here, I already have your name and will know it when I see what room you go to. What. Is. Your. Name?"

"Sorry again, what was that?" asked Ben, climbing the stairs to his room.

"Why is my pool SMOKING?"

Ben broke into a run at this, shouting one last "I'm sorry, what?" Laura, the only innocent in the entire escapade, was left holding the bag – literally, as in the bag of dry ice. She hung her head as the owner turned on her.

"Do you know that joker?"

Laura sighed. "Yes, he's my boss."

Laura then proceeded to explain that it was a small bit of dry ice in the pool, and we would have checked with her but didn't want to wake her, and gave a very convincing, scientific-sounding explanation for why it wasn't dangerous to have dry ice in the pool. The owner was not convinced. The rules had been broken and someone needed to be punished. That someone, she had decided correctly, was Ben. Laura offered all kinds of deals, but it was no use.

We watched as they marched to Ben's room, knocked on the door, waited, knocked again, waited, threatened to get the master key, before Ben opened the door. Here is another reason why I love Ben – he had just been caught swimming in a speedo and throwing dry ice into the pool, the woman had seen him, up close, spoken with him, and watched him go into his room, but he still answered the door as if she and Laura had just woken him from a deep sleep. He had changed into boxer shorts and was attempting to speak while yawning and stretching as if he'd been asleep the whole time. The acting was incredible, but slightly hindered by the fact that he was still dripping wet. We couldn't exactly hear what was being said, but it was evident that the owner was angry. A few minutes later, Ben and Laura were heading to the van, escorted by the owner, and driving away. She glanced in the direction of Robin's room and we saw a flutter of curtains and heard James' loud laugh. After watching the owner go back to her quarters – James, Robin, Dom, and I crept out of our rooms and met outside of the pool.

"What do you think happened? Did they get kicked out? What should we do? I've tried calling both of their cells and they either don't have them or they're turned off."

We determined there was nothing we could do for the time being so we stood around and watched the smoke slowly rising from the pool. "It really is beautiful, isn't it?" asked James. "Would have made such a great shot."

Laura came back about 30 minutes later. "Ben's at a different hotel. We'll talk about this in the morning, boys." She said in her best mom voice. Cowed, we all went to our respective rooms.

In the morning, Laura instructed each of us to go and apologize to the owner for our roles in the previous night's mayhem. We did. By the time it was my turn, she was laughing about the whole thing and saying that she may have overreacted. It seemed Laura had impressed her. It looked like all was forgiven, but Ben was still nowhere to be seen. Laura was letting him sleep in a little, she said. She then went to pick him up, and it was Ben's turn to apologize on his return. Once he left the owner's office, we all asked what had happened. All we got from Ben was, "I had to sleep in the naughty hotel."

Laura replied, "Yes, you did. You were bad so you had to sleep in the bad hotel." It turned out that the owner had been planning to call the police, and the negotiated compromise was that Ben would leave and we would prove the pool was safe to swim in. Laura drove Ben around town looking for any hotel with a "vacancy" sign. The one she found had no AC and only one tiny room above a garage – the naughty hotel. She had also woken up early and tracked down pool chemistry kits to show the water was safe. Laura is the best.

We had a light filming schedule that day, which was one of the reasons we had felt OK about staying up until the wee hours to play Kabaddi, swim, film re-enactments, etc the night before. We only needed a few shots on the beach and some productions stills. The beach shots were basically just me giving my thoughts about the trip and sea serpents in general to the camera. They usually used bits and pieces of this throughout the episode. Essentially, the cameraman would start filming and I would rant and ramble while they switched angles, positions, etc. Robin started rolling and I started talking. The sun was high and we were all pretty spent from the night before. We quickly decided to do this one sitting down. After a few minutes, I noticed the camera drooping to one side, then Robin fell over, asleep, camera on his shoulder. It felt like the perfect ending for this debacle of a shoot.

Chapter 3

# "If They Try to Hurt You, I Won't Be Able to Help, but I Will Get It on Film"

## ... and Other Stories That Prove a Stranger's Just a Friend You Haven't Met

When asked to be on a TV show, most people are a little nervous, but excited. The crew of the Ocean Pearl fishing vessel were not most people. For them, appearing on *Beast Hunter* meant an extra two days tacked onto a trip which had already taken them away from their families for six weeks, no additional money in their pockets, and five "flatlanders" on board (one a lady) with all of the bad juju that comes along with them. As I climbed onto the boat, I saw a sea of very rough, unshaven, angry faces. I was more uncomfortable and intimidated than the first time I met my in-laws.

It didn't help that in the week leading up to our two-night black-cod fishing excursion, Ben kept telling me how rough the crew was and how angry they were that we were joining them.

"These guys are tough, man, I mean it. Long haul fisherman. They've been at sea for nearly two months *and* we're delaying their return to their families. I bet they'll blame you, TV's Pat Spain. You know, if they try to hurt you, I won't be able to help, but I promise we'll get it on film. Right, Robin? Then press charges later..." And so on.

We were in British Columbia investigating stories of a sea serpent named Caddy. We'd been having extraordinarily good luck finding credible, kind, and accommodating witnesses on this shoot. Our interactions with locals were generally positive experiences – there was the occasional blowhard or person that was clearly lying to get on TV, but this was one of the best parts of a really fun job. The witnesses in BC had been exceptional.

There were a couple of guys who had spent their whole lives on the water. Our interviews with them occurred in some of the most picturesque spots in British Columbia – think evergreen-covered jagged-rock cliffs overlooking pristine bays. There was a boat builder who welcomed us onto his land, introduced us to his black labs, and gave us free range to explore and film anything we wanted. He had a barn that was over 200 years old where I happily caught a bunch of garter snakes and fence lizards, and there was a pair of very wealthy women who welcomed us with open arms into one of their lavish homes – literally open arms, waiting to hug us all. They had prepared a spread of bagels, muffins, coffee, and tea (as they'd heard that British people like tea) that would have put any hotel's continental breakfast to shame. We ate breakfast and lunch (homemade salads, sandwiches, and grilled fare also provided by them) on their deck, and between filming interviews with them were given leave to fully explore their gorgeous waterfront property, catch sea creatures, and encouraged to play fetch with their impossible-not-to-love yellow lab. This was such a refreshing change from our normal intake of take-out, gas-station coffee, and rest-area bathrooms.

We were also given the incredible opportunity to spend a couple of days with BC's First Nations tribes, whom I awkwardly (and maybe with a little subconscious jingoism) kept referring to as Native Americans. BC, like much of the New World, has a long, sordid, and embarrassing history with the native peoples who were present well before white folks "discovered" their lands. Unlike much of America, however, BC seems to actively be trying to right old wrongs, and regularly restores lands of cultural and historic importance to tribes. While we were there, a burial mound was discovered in downtown Nanaimo and the First Nations successfully petitioned to have the land turned over to them. It was heartening to see a government taking steps to recognize centuries of unfair treatment of millions of people.

Many First Nations tribes live on reservations in BC. We visited one that was the home of the Snuneymuxw People (pronounce Snah-nay-mux). It looked like a middle-class suburb and was positioned on a gorgeous bay. It was a beautiful spring day and many of the adults were gathered on their decks, grilling, talking, and laughing. We saw groups of disaffected teenagers playing games, skateboarding, or huddled together gossiping. The only thing that made them stand out from any other mall-going, angst-ridden kids was the disproportionate number of *Twilight* T-shirts – it seemed that three out of four kids had a Jacob shirt, bag, hoodie, or some other paraphernalia. According to our guide and liaison in the First Nations lands, *Twilight* had been a boon for these kids, who finally had a Native pop-culture icon. I'm sure Taylor Lautner's abs didn't hurt his status as their current idol either.

Our guide was Xul Si' Malt (pronounced Hahl See Mahl), a soft-spoken older man who exuded kindness and wisdom. He was balding and the hair he had was mostly gray with a little black mixed in. He was one of those guys where the graying and balding made him appear distinguished and wise, someone with experience. He had a deeply lined face and very strong, leathery hands. He was solid and muscular, like a football player. When he smiled his entire face wrinkled and lit up as his eyes disappeared into the folds around them. His voice was not deep, but resonant, like you'd imagine it would be as he was the storyteller of his people, and his mission was to preserve the language, customs, and tales of the Snuneymuxw. He greeted us warmly, welcomed us to their traditional lands, and, when we asked how he would prefer to be addressed, said, "Call me Gary."

Gary told us all about the fight to preserve his people's ways and lands. I hope by the above paragraphs I didn't imply that the BC government was simply turning land over – it was a fight, but one that the Native People's seemed to be winning more often than not. Gary showed us ancient petroglyphs and spoke of secret rituals and rites that he still conducted in an unbroken chain dating back to time immemorial. He said: "Most teenagers in our tribe when I was younger thought this stuff was boring; they wanted to assimilate. I am proud to have kept it alive for the new generation, who seem eager to reconnect with their heritage." He ran a sort of after-school club, and was happy to say attendance was way up. Gary also started nearly every story with, "In the beginning of time," which seemed to be where his voice emanated from as he got into his tales. It was amazing and inspiring to speak with him.

Gary invited us to his family's house for a ceremony to welcome spring. They and a few friends were on his deck overlooking the bay, all dressed in jeans and T-shirts. Gary was dressed similarly but had traditional face paint, drums, and various feathered headdresses laid out. He invited us to join in, and his wife (who was clearly humoring him, but seemed to enjoy how much he enjoyed this) painted us and presented us with the headdresses. I, stupidly, put it on "feathers at the back" style, a-la "Native Americans in American Westerns." This elicited a lot of laughs from the assembled crowd and a weary smile from Gary. "I'd like to meet the American who first put a headdress on an actor in this way."

"You'd like to punch him you mean," said his smiling wife. Feathers go in the front – millions of Thanksgiving plays are wrong – shocking I know. With painted faces, traditional drums in hand, and headdresses appropriately donned, we repeated after Gary and chanted/sang to the eagles, who would "carry our song over the mountains and into the sky." Gary's wife presented a few different foil-wrapped salmons, saying, "I think we should have probably caught these from the streams for this to be official, but, Stop-n-Shop works on short notice." Gary blessed the fish and it was held up to our mouths so that we could eat some without using our hands (as we were instructed to do) A portion was set aside, and Gary told us his friend would drive it to a ceremonial location and leave it for the eagles.

I've participated in many tribal ceremonies all over the world, but this one seemed somehow the most earnest. Despite the suburban setting, the jeans, and T-shirts, with the upbeat, spring BBQ-type feel, it seemed to mean the most to the people leading it. Gary really loved the traditions of his people, and was proud to be continuing them and passing them on to new generations. Nothing about it felt forced, or flippant, or played up for the cameras. Unlike the Adidas-wearing tribes in West Africa who would don a grass skirt when the cameras turned on, or the shaman who seemed to be playing a role rather than "owning" this tradition, this felt like all participants fully engaged in the ceremony and meaning behind the rituals.

We left Gary's house with some extra salmon for the long trip up the coast to the location we would be meeting the Ocean Pearl. That night, Ben skyped his family back in Bristol to tell them about the salmon ceremony. His boys, aged 2 and 4 at the time, had many questions for him. "Daddy, do they wear pants in Canada?" was the primary one. They also wondered if people "ate food." Ben replied in the affirmative to both, and decided that they might be a bit young to really grasp the beauty of what we had done that day.

We stayed in a not-to-be-named chain hotel on the night before the boat trip, and arranged to put a fair amount of our gear in storage for the few nights we'd be gone so we didn't have to lug everything onto the boat. We also stole the pillows from our rooms because we had all forgotten to pack any of our own. I don't remember whose idea it was, but we decided it would be fun to smuggle them out in bizarre ways. Laura just put hers in her luggage, like a sane person. Ben brazenly kept his under his arm and ignored the concerned looks from hotel workers who were clearly struggling with whether to say anything to him or not. I wasn't going to take mine, but caved under peer pressure and, after checking out, asked for my key back, ran into my room and grabbed the pillow, shoved about half of it into a backpack, then ran straight to the car past the frowning concierge, feeling like I'd just robbed a bank. James had the best method. He shoved the pillow under his shirt and remarked loudly about how full he was the entire time we were checking out. Laura called us all idiots and threatened to deduct the cost of the pillows from our pay if the hotel charged us for them.

On the way to the boats, we found out that Nat Geo had officially decided on the name of the series. Up until this point we had been using the working title *Wild Thing*. Ben announced that my first big TV series on Nat Geo – the thing I'd been dreaming about since I was in diapers, the thing I'd spent every dime and every spare minute working towards for the past six years – would be called... *Beast Hunter*. *Beast Man* in the UK. When we submitted the list of potential names, Barny added those two as a sort of afterthought. I think they rounded the list up to 20 names, or something like that. Never did any of us imagine that they'd be picked. The names were fine, and people much more skilled at this kind of thing had picked them, but we were so used to *Wild Thing* that it felt strange. Ben renamed the show *Pat Spain: Monster Puncher*, and came up with the tagline: "First he shows science that these animals exist, then he shows these animals who's boss." This devolved into *Monster Kicker* – "Pat Spain finds legendary creatures, and kicks them where it hurts."

We arrived at the docks and were greeted by the ship's captain, who told us that due to the unusual tides we weren't going to leave until the next day. He invited us to join him and the first mate for dinner at a local restaurant. We asked if the rest of the crew would be meeting us there and he, a little awkwardly, explained that they would be staying on the boat because they "wanted to be ready to leave as soon as possible." This very clearly meant they were angry. Picking us up had now added four days onto their already lengthy stay at sea, and they didn't want to be in our presence any longer than they absolutely needed to. On top of this, we would now be eating at a nice restaurant while they sulked on the boat all night, alone. I didn't see how this could possibly go wrong.

Early the next morning, Ben suggested we film my getting on the boat with a long lens first, meaning the crew would be about 500 yards away from me and I would board alone. One of the "fun" things about filming with a single camera is that you need to repeat every action, conversation, and experience at least three times using a long lens, a wide lens, and from different perspectives (yours or the person you are talking to – generally both). Most people laugh when you explain this to them. For some reason, I didn't think the crew of the ship would find it amusing. I was right.

I asked Ben if James or Laura could come with me to explain this to the guys, or at least distract them from taking their anger out on me. Ben explained that they needed to get me walking the whole way to the ship, and if Laura or James boarded before me there was a risk of accidentally getting them in the shot, which would further delay the already angry crew. "And we wouldn't want to do that, would we?" said Ben. So, I walked to the boat alone and climbed onboard – incorrectly it turned out. I didn't use the normal entry point, which was the first of many foibles that put us all in danger according to fisherman superstitions.

I boarded, grinning like an idiot, and six very scruffy, red, and angry faces turned towards me.

"FUCK! Fine! About fucking time. Can we fucking leave now?" This was from a man named Bull who was wrapping a length of rope around his arm, and was immediately followed by, "This is so fucking stupid. I want to go *home*. Do you fucking get it? Can we fucking leave now? FUCK!" from Ryan, who was pacing back and forth, looking very much like a caged animal.

"Where are the other assholes? Can you get them on the fucking boat so we can fucking leave? NOW!?!?" said Bull.

Under my breath, into my lapel mic, I said, "Um guys, please come on board right away. They are very angry and want to leave immediately."

"Hey, guys!" I said to the crew. "My name's Pat. Thanks so much for letting us join you. I know it's kind of a pain in the ass." I approached one of them with my hand out. No one shook it.

"Seriously, get those fucks on board," said Ryan.

"Um, actually, it's kind of a funny thing with filming. We need to film me boarding a couple more times from different angles. I know it's weird, but the guys will be coming down as soon as they can carry all the gear. Maybe I should go help them, actually." I looked up and saw James, our sound tech, waving his arms, motioning for me to stay on the boat. "Um, no, never mind, I'll just stay here. I'm sure they'll be right down."

"You have to board a few times? Are we just supposed to stand here and watch every time like assholes? Why didn't you need to film me boarding? What, am I just going to magically fucking appear on a boat? Why do they only need to see you getting on? You didn't even board right. Next time they film you, do it right. Over here, see?" He pointed to the very obvious entrance to the boat which I had somehow missed.

I nervously laughed a little, then said, "Um, if I board over there, it won't look the same in the other shots as the first one, and we'd have to do the whole thing over."

"I don't give a shit. It's bad luck to board how you did. You're not doing it another 40 goddam times and getting 40 goddam more times of goddam bad luck."

"James," I said into my lapel mic, "please tell Ben they are very angry but probably won't assault me."

"Are you and your show pro or anti-fishing?" asked Bull.

"Um, pro?"

"I'm anti-fishing. We murder the sea, you know."

"James, strike that, please get here immediately."

I repeated my initial boarding, the right way this time, then boarded "40 more goddam times," was finally joined by the crew, and the boat pushed off. As we passed some sealions I started spouting off some useless facts about them within earshot of Bull, who said, "We hate those fuckers because they eat our fish, but we can't shoot them." Then he laughed and said, "Just kidding. But we do hate them. Tell me more about 'um."

I gave him not just the sealion but all the marine mammal facts I knew, and by the time I got to my favorite – Blue whales have 16-foot penises and testicles the size of VW Beetles – Bull and I were fast friends. I similarly bonded with the rest of the crew over my Cliff Clavin-esque knowledge of marine life's bizarre sexual facts and other random wildlife stories. After I showed a scar from my rabid raccoon attack and Ryan compared it to one of his fishing scars, I realized all was forgiven for our delaying them. They turned out to be a really funny, smart, and kind group of guys who had just wanted to play up the biases they'd correctly assumed we'd had about them and mess with us for a bit.

Liam was a fellow marine biologist in training, an undergrad student working the fishing boats to make extra money. He was an Irishman with black hair and light blue eyes. His angular face was beet red, as if he was perpetually blushing. Laura, being of a pale complexion herself, made a joke about Irish skin and sunblock. Liam pretended to have no idea what she was talking about, saying, "I was born this red, it's a birth defect. Thanks for bringing it up," before finally breaking and laughing, saying he probably already had cancer from the amount of sun he'd taken in. One of the coolest things he told me was that he'd spotted a live giant squid off the side of the boat a year before.

Scooby was third in command after Captain Mike and first mate, Darcy. He was incredibly friendly and kind of a hippy. He said the only thing he didn't like about being out at sea was how much he missed his family, but in every other way he loved it out there. Despite his job, he was totally against killing animals, and when off the boat loved to garden and cook. He told me that when he retires, he will never kill another fish or animal.

Jimmy was the chef and had one of the best mustaches this side of Tom Selleck. He was a huge personality on a very skinny frame. He was proud of his job, and rightfully so. The man could *cook*. It wasn't easy to keep this group of guys happy, day in and day out, and food was a huge part of that. While we were on the boat, he made us a couple of the best meals I can remember, including some tiger shrimp and black-cod cheeks that we caught ourselves.

Bull and Ryan both had baby faces beneath their massive beards. All the guys shaved on our last day, rendering them virtually unrecognizable, but none as much as Ryan. With no beard, Bull looked exactly like the lead singer of one of my favorite bands, The Bronx. It was uncanny. Both Bull and Ryan loved/missed their families a lot. They were both great guys and started teasing me about how scared I'd been when we first met. I'm lucky to have met all of these guys.

That first night on the ship, The Icon crew and I were laughing about not being able to walk straight due to the ship's rocking motion, our misconceptions about the fisherman, and our stolen hotel pillows. The guys started filling us in on all the superstitions of sailing. Some we'd heard, such as the bad luck associated with having a woman on board, but others were new to us. A rule against whistling seemed bizarre, but the extreme disdain showed for anyone who "opened a can upside down" just seemed unnecessary. Has anyone ever opened a can upside down? How would you even do that? Our answer was that we shouldn't even be talking about it.

Jimmy advised us to pop some Dramamine, saying, "By the time you feel like you need it, it's too late." Ben wisely listened to him, having had a bad experience on a fishing boat years before. The rest of us laughed it off, claiming we'd already gotten our sea legs. After hearing Robin claim he doesn't get seasick, Mike said, "Everyone gets seasick, you just haven't yet."

We turned in at around 10 pm as we were planning to wake up at 4 am so we could be there with the guys on deck as they started hauling in traps that would hopefully be filled with black cod. They guys worked 16-hour shifts, so they gave the four of us our own bunk room (Laura was sleeping in the ladies' quarters, otherwise known as a storage closet on deck). The bunk room was very narrow and the beds tiny – it was like sleeping in a RV or a sleeper car on a train. I had the top bunk and drifted off to sleep to the gentle rolling of the waves and the sound of the engine. I woke up about an hour later convinced the room was on fire. It wasn't, but it was about 97 degrees in there. I immediately stripped down to boxers and noticed everyone else had done the same. We understood why this entire bunk room was unused.

I woke up again at around 3:45 feeling distinctly unwell. The ship was rocking in an alarming way, and James, who had been his normal chipper self the night before, looked literally green faced. Ben was a little pale but seemed okay. Robin was holding his head like he had the worst hangover of his life. And when we exited the cabin, Laura was already leaning overboard, puking. The site of this brought James to the edge of the boat to also lose his supper.

James and Laura tried to continue their respective jobs, but spent a fair amount of the next hour vomiting on each other due to blowback as they switched places leaning over the deck. As I put on my borrowed deck gear (giant thermal and waterproof pants, boots, jacket, gloves, etc.), I asked Bull if the seas got rougher than this. He laughed and told me this was considered "flat." I almost puked right then. After filming a quick piece to camera, Ben told James to take some meds and go back to sleep. We didn't see him for another 12 hours. Laura insisted she could power through it, and after an hour in the fetal position in her "room" was back on deck looking reasonably healthy. She is tough as nails, that lady.

Ryan told me that looking at the horizon helps with nausea, and, as the sun came up and I stared at that fixed line in the distance, I actually started feeling better. I had made it past the initial nausea without puking and was now challenged with standing upright on a rocking, slippery ship as waves crashed over the sides. The waves seemed huge to me, *Deadliest Catch*-style, and one nearly took Scooby out as he wrestled with a winch. The wave knocked him just as the wench loosed and he swung overboard, holding onto the rope until the rocking brought him safely over the deck again. Ben, Robin, Laura, and I paled with concern and shock, but the crew just took it in their stride, barely even mentioning the fact that Scooby almost died. This was apparently just part of normal life aboard a fishing vessel. They still claimed these were "calm" seas. I can't imagine being out there at the end of a 16-hour shift, in the dark, in rough seas.

Work on the boat was terrifying, demanding, fast, and fascinating. There is no way I would live long enough to collect a paycheck, but some of the guys told me they are able to make a year's pay in four months and spend the next eight with their families. Some supplement with odd jobs like painting, others just garden and hang out when they're not on the water. The captain and first mate shoulder the financial burden, making sure they can pay the crew, the lease on the boat, maintenance fees, etc. Mike and Darcy were great guys – very knowledgeable, friendly, funny, etc. – but more serious than the rest of the crew. They had to be. They had started as a black-cod fishing vessel, but with the weather and catch getting less predictable have been forced into other areas of fishing to pay the bills. We heard similar stories all over the world – people being forced to adapt to conditions outside of their control. I saw a "dry" season in Sumatra that consisted of a 13-day torrential downpour, fishermen in West Africa who hadn't caught a large fish in years, hunter/gatherers in the Central African Republic who had become guides because there wasn't enough to hunt and gather, and nomads in Mongolia who noticed the seasons shifting in unpredictable ways. The times they are a-changing, and the easiest way to really see this, Westerners, is to travel to less moderate regions of the world.

Back to the boat, and we were hauling up traps the guys had laid the night before. Each one was like unwrapping a Christmas present for my marine-bio self! The by-catch was far more exciting to me than a trap filled to the gills with black cod. We caught viperfish, bizarre bottom-dwelling crabs, jellyfish of all sorts, squid, odd inverts including huge shrimp the size of lobsters, and tons of hagfish. Hagfish are one of the most bizarre animals on Earth. Their closest relative is a lamprey, but just how close is a heated debate amongst us nerds. While I wasn't allowed to say it on Nat Geo (because we couldn't back it up with enough sources), there is some debate as to whether they should even be classified as "fish" due to their lack of a jaw and vertebral column. They are the only animal that intentionally ties itself in a knot as a means of eating and to escape from predators, and they produce excessive amounts of very thick, gelatinous slime when threatened. The fishermen hated them because if one hagfish made its way into a trap, chances were, it would eat all of the encased fish from the inside out by the time they hauled them on deck, and all that would be left were fish-shaped bags of skin and bones with a fat hagfish inside one of them. I loved catching and playing with them, though.

After killing, heading, and gutting a half dozen fish, I had managed to stab myself, stab Jimmy, and cut one fish incorrectly, rendering it unusable for market. I was also so sore later that I could barely move my arms. I can't imagine processing hundreds of fish in a 16-hour shift the way these guys do. After seeing my "skills" they relegated me to cutting the cheeks out of fish heads. The cheeks are the tastiest part of the fish, but there isn't much of a market demand for them. The guys told me that, if they have time, they cut a few hundred for friends and restaurants that they know like them. They also take them for themselves and Jimmy cooks them up for dinner.

The steady stream of by-catch, guts, heads, and spines behind the boat meant that we had an entourage of seabirds and the occasional dolphin pod. It was really cool watching the dolphins swim alongside the boat, and the birds were interesting also. The guys called the albatrosses "goofy birds" because of the way they seemed to run along the water with their wings out, looking awkward and gawky. There was nothing goofy about them in the air, though. They are one of the most proficient gliders on Earth and soar with an otherworldly grace. They represented yet another seeming contradiction out there on the open water.

After pulling back into dock we shook hands with all the crew members and wished them luck. Some of their wives/girlfriends/kids were waiting for them in the parking lot, and it was remarkable to see all the gruffness of the past few days just melt away as they embraced each other and became their "normal" selves. Bull stopped before getting off the boat and told me that I had good sea legs "for a flatlander." It was one of the nicest compliments paid to me during the entire series.

After the boat ride and just before leaving Canada, we stopped at the hotel to pick up our stuff and return the pillows. Laura again drew the short straw and had the thankless task of explaining how we ended up with five of the hotel's pillows, and arguing that we shouldn't be charged any more than a "rental" fee. Robin's idea was to put them all in a rolling bin and pretend we had locked them up with the rest of our gear. Not a bad suggestion – better than the idea from James and myself of "throw them behind the concierge desk and run away." Laura decided instead to simply explain that we had all "accidentally" packed them and we were now righting our mistake. Amazingly it worked, and we were thanked for returning them. Film crews – we make friends everywhere we go. Or maybe, more accurately: Canadians – the nicest people on Earth.

## Chapter 4

# Caddy: "Is anyone here a Marine Biologist?"

Here be Dragons.
(Hunt-Lennox Globe)

Hello there and thank you for making it this far with me. We've come to the "cryptid" – or mysterious animals that may or may not exist – chapter of the book. This is either a very weird turn in the funny travel book you've been enjoying, or you were *very* confused by the first few chapters of the cryptozoology book you purchased. I will not be citing my sources here (most of them are my own notes and memories anyway). Feel free to Google anything I mention and write angry emails and nasty tweets about how I got the volume of the ocean wrong. This is not a paper in a scientific journal. It's a collection of true stories from my personal experiences, and some of my opinions. When making *Beast Hunter*, we needed to cite at least two credited (peer-reviewed or expert-opinion) sources for every fact I stated on camera. There was a fact checker at Nat Geo whose job was to pick apart every line said. Most networks do not require this, but it's one of the reasons I love Nat Geo so much and why it's among the most respected brands in the world. This did make our job of making films about animals that may or may not exist very difficult. There were so many retakes in order to throw in a "perhaps" or a "some experts say" that we ended up doing a five-minute reel of me just repeating phrases that imply ambiguity in different intonations which we could cut in during editing. In fact we loved the scrutiny, and I feel it made the series much better than your run-of-the-mill crypto show filled with statements like "that's definitely a werewolf" when someone hears a barred owl; or an episode with more night-vision footage than a wannabe actor's "break-out" video (regardless of whether the proposed animal is nocturnal or not) and lots of loud noises and Blair Witch-style nausea-inducing camera movements followed by "What's *THAT?!?*", or – in my opinion, the biggest crime in this field – faked news stories or actors playing scientists. That is bullshit, I say!

There were a few things in *Beast Hunter* that were cut by our fact checker which I would still argue were true. We had to lose most of the aforementioned hagfish segment because I said, "They aren't closely related to anything else, and they really aren't even a fish by a strict definition." I *may* have slightly overstated how different they are evolutionarily, but I maintain that what I said was true. (My friend Zeb, a real marine biologist, is probably cringing reading this.) It's that kind of scrutiny and adherence to the truth that I think set our show apart. Anyway, there is no fact checker on this book, other than you, dear reader. So, check away, but as I said – these are mostly my own thoughts, opinions, and experiences.

In case you haven't figured it out yet, I am a nerd. Not like "I went to see Avatar twice! I'm such a NERD!", like a real nerd. And specifically, a science nerd. This differs from the so-hot-right-now comic-book/sci-fi nerd. Sure, I liked *Fringe* as much as the next guy, I've read all of the *Song of Ice and Fire* books to date, and my high-school friends and I stayed in on Friday nights to watch *X-Files*, but my true nerd status really becomes apparent whenever a conversation strays into any topic in biology. I advocated for the name Darwin if our first child was a boy, and, when we found out we were having a daughter, tried to convince Anna it would still make a great middle name. We ended up naming our daughter Luna after the amazingly beautiful and mysterious *Actias luna*, the luna moth. (Yes, I'm aware that Luna Lovegood is a character in one of my favorite books' series. She's one of Anna's and my favorite characters, in fact. That was, however, an added bonus for the name rather than a driving force.) Our son is named Wallace Charles after Alfred Russel Wallace, Charles Darwin, and Charles Fort. I was a teaching assistant for multiple chemistry and biology labs, and audited extra biology and philosophy classes – for fun. I traveled to Maryland to observe horseshoe crabs mating – again, for fun. One of the only real fights I can remember getting into with my best friend, whom I've been friends with since birth, was when we were eight and he insisted that crabs were amphibians. The only TV shows I watched in the eighties and nineties were nature programs. Whenever I was home sick from school, I was allowed to rent anything I wanted from the video store. My pick was always a volume of *Life on Earth*. David Attenborough, Alfred Russel Wallace, and Charles Darwin were my childhood heroes, and remain my adult heroes – in addition to Harry Marshall, the co-founder of Icon Films.

When I moved out of my house at 16 and lived on my own for the first time, it was for a marine bio internship in Maine. A friend asked what the nightlife was like in southern Maine. I replied with no hesitation or sense of irony, "Great! It's really awesome! There are foxes, raccoons, lightning bugs, polyphemus moths, and so far, I've spotted two species of owls!" I also read the *Fortean Times* and *Cryptozoonews*, and most of the people I follow on social media are naturalists. Don't worry, though – I won't get *too* scientific in this chapter (and there will be poop jokes).

I say all of this because, in recent years, there has been a move toward hijacking nerd culture by moderately cool people. An actor who can't quite cut it turns to fantasy shows and suddenly he's a heartthrob. A few years back, even Charlie Sheen "led a search for the Loch Ness Monster." I happened to be in Scotland, investigating the same monster at the same time, and heard some horror stories from the locals about his behavior in their beautiful country. I am not a person who does this stuff for the attention – I do it because I love it, am fascinated by it, and think it doesn't do science any favours to simply write off the things that sound bizarre.

Too many scientists forget that the general public does not consist primarily of other scientists, and that most people would rather hear about the *possibility* of a bipedal intelligent ape walking through the Great North Woods than the reality of the new barnacle you discovered. Run with that – talk about the *possibility* of things that people, real people, will find interesting, and get them listening. Then throw in some stuff about wolverines, the reintroduction of wolves, and pine martens. Tell some jokes, give some sexy facts – more people would be interested in your lame barnacle if you led with the fact that it has the largest penis to body ratio of any animal in the world. It's over six times the total length of its body! Don't refuse to talk about something because you think it sounds silly. Getting people outside for a homemade Bigfoot expedition still gets them outside, and they *will* see other amazing and exciting things, even if they don't see a sasquatch. A generation of Bigfoot hunters might turn into conservationists, or field biologists, or maybe lawyers who will want to protect the land they loved exploring as a kid. Another interesting side effect of not immediately writing these things off, all of you closed-minded scientists out there, is that sometimes, *sometimes*, you might find that there is actually *something* to these stories. If you go out there, use your scientific training, open your mind, dispel disbelief and really look at the facts and evidence, you might surprise yourself, like I did with Caddy in BC, and others.

I'm an open-minded skeptic at heart, and I approached everything around *Beast Hunter* as such. There's a famous quote regarding Occam's Razor that goes something like, "When you hear hoof beats in the distance, you don't think it's a herd of unicorns. You think of horses, and you're probably correct." I also think of horses, but am willing to be shown the evidence of unicorns. I had a "mistaken identity" theory for each cryptid we covered on the show, and was more interested in the cultural significance of each myth than its veracity. But Caddy? I have to admit that, before the expedition, I was 99% sure there is a real animal behind it. Now I'm 99.99% sure. I just don't think you'll be as excited as me when we find it.

This was the expedition that, selfishly, I was the *most* excited for. *Cadborosaurus willsi*, or Caddy, is a legendary species of sea serpent often spotted in the Pacific Northwest – particularly in British Columbia. As a "marine biologist" and crypto-enthusiast, I was well versed in all the theories about what Caddy might be. I had my own pet theory as well – we'll get into that later. I had thought through all of the possible mistaken identities and had prepared answers to questions from critics. I was convinced that, even though we were unlikely to find one, we could show scientifically that Caddy was real. We'd do this by showing what *else* was in the ocean that we know about, and point out just how much we still have to learn. I'll carry that even further here and really indulge my inner nerd.

## The Ocean

Okay, let's just get it out there – the ocean is *weird*. Like, really weird, and brimming with truly bizarre animals. Oh, and it's mysterious. So mysterious that we know next to nothing about its inhabitants. We are talking about an unfathomably (pun intended) large area of our world – 139 million square miles, give or take, with a volume of 310 million cubic miles. There are an estimated 2 million marine species, of which we've only named about 230,000 – and they are 230,000 of the freakiest, most Sci-fi-movie-monster looking animals ever. I'll just mention a few of my favorites.

Google "giant deep-sea isopod" and get ready to have nightmares about huge flesh-eating bugs. Or their even creepier relative, the giant tongue-eating louse, which eats a fish's tongue (as its name would imply) and then latches onto the stump and begins its new life as *the fish's new tongue*. How about a gulper eel? It's a fish with a black stomach to block the bioluminescent light from its prey – which is often *larger* than the eel itself, and consumed whole then digested slowly while they are still alive. What about the goblin shark, whose jaws shoot from its mouth in a terrifying accordion-esque projectile of two-inch-long nail-like teeth? Or a siphonophore – a giant colonial organism that's like a living, 150-foot-long spider's web made of stinging cells? How about everyone's favorite character from *Finding Nemo*, the deep-sea angler fish? The males are tiny compared to the females and bite her, parasitizing and eventually embedding themselves in her flesh where they stay for the rest of their lives, sharing a circulatory system and just releasing sperm whenever she needs it (insert joke about all males being sperm-donating parasites here). What about a vampire squid? Or, better yet, a giant squid – or, even *better*, a *colossal* squid! *Or* the *best*, a Ginormous squid! Okay, I made up that last one, but really, any deep-sea squid, they are all equally terrifying and fascinating, and have awesome names. You don't get much weirder or more mysterious than squids.

The giant squid is my favorite animal, and it's what hooked me into marine biology in the first place. (So. Many. Bio-puns. Buckle-up.) Imagine a 40-foot, highly intelligent and aggressive animal that was only documented alive in 2012. They are only a couple of inches long at birth, but reach their massive size within a few short years – it's believed they only live about five. We know next to nothing definitive about them. We also don't know how many species of giant squid there are, or if we've yet found the biggest or weirdest. In fact, nearly all of our knowledge about these massive creatures comes from a few dozen dead and decaying ones found washed up on beaches around the world.

We are constantly finding new, giant, and bizarre marine

life. Megamouth sharks are one of the largest species of shark (reaching about 18 feet in length) and were not discovered until 1976. Since then, only around 50 have been found. New species of beaked whales are still being discovered today, and they are mammals – whales, in fact! They have to come to the surface to breath. The surface is about the only part of the ocean we know anything about, and even there we are finding new animals. Would anyone be surprised if we found the NTIs from *The Abyss* in some deep trench in the pacific? I wouldn't.

Why do I mention all of this in a chapter that's supposed to be about a sea serpent? Well, it's to show you that the *known* animals in the ocean sound like you're making them up, and to illustrate that we are constantly finding new ones. Nothing coming from the deep sea should surprise us, so a sea serpent? Yeah, absolutely. Why not?

I could pull a Charles Fort and just leave it at that. A lot has been written about sea monsters, and even conservative marine biologists believe there are large undiscovered animals in the ocean, so no need to go any further, right? Well, that wouldn't be much fun. Let's speculate, shall we? Let's start with Solow and Smith's 2005 paper from the Royal Biologics Society which used a statistical analysis of animal discovery rates in the twentieth century to predict (did you fall asleep there? It's okay, I understand – don't worry, this gets weirder) that there are upwards of 16 large (over six feet long) marine vertebrates left to be discovered. Paxton used a similar technique and put the number in the 30s to 50s. Raynal predicted 15 cetaceans (whales and dolphins), and most recently Dr. Darren Naish put the approximate number of undiscovered pinnipeds (seals, sea lions, and walruses) at three. So, we're looking at a few pinnipeds, some more cetaceans, and quite a few "others." Then let's speculate about which would be the most likely explanation for all the Caddy sightings? That would be fun, right? I'll break this chapter down into the usual suspects and try to rank the likelihood that these creatures are Caddy, then finally give my own take and completely unsubstantiated theories.

## Caddy

First, some background on *Cadborosaurus willsi* (the creature was preemptively given a Latin name by Bousfield and LeBlond in 1995, but I will use "Caddy" from here on out, as it's shorter and catchy). It was named for Cadboro Bay off of Vancouver Island where a number of sightings of the creature have been reported. Caddy is not an officially recognized species, and even ardent believers admit it is likely that sightings represent multiple species – some known, some potentially unknown. In the last 200 years there have been over 300 reportedly credible sightings of a creature meeting the following description:

- Size: 6–60 feet long
- Body type: elongated, tubular, with a tree-trunk-like thickness; number of fins differ by account from none to two on the front of its body, to multiple sets running its entire length
  - Some accounts describe a long, thin neck, with a more robust body, loch-ness monster style
- Skin: Scaly or smooth/shiny; some reports include a crest or fin running along its back
- Head: horse or camel-like. Some reports include protrusions on top of the head, with small bumps like the knobby ossicones of a giraffe or okapi
- Habitat: unknown marine environment – theorized to be the deep ocean; sightings occur along the Pacific Coast of North America and seem most prevalent in the waters of British Columbia (although sea serpent sighting occurs the world over)
- Diet: reports of it eating fish and sea birds
- Temperament: most reports indicate that it is not

aggressive
- Kingdom, phylum, class, order, family, genus, or species: unknown. Theories include mistaken identity for a known, or potentially unknown, type of:
  - reptile (snake, crocodile, turtle – you know what reptiles are, I hope)
  - pinniped (seal, sealion – furry marine mammals)
  - cetacean (whales/dolphins – non-furry marine mammals)
  - cephalopod (squid, octopus, nautilus, cuttlefish)
  - osteichthyes (bony fish – not sharks or rays)
  - chondrichthyes (sharks, rays, skates)
  - cervidae (deer and deer-like mammals)
  - aves (birds)
  ...and just about every other type of animal that you can imagine.

There is a long and rich oral history of a creature meeting this description amongst the First Nations tribes in Canada. There are ancient carvings and paintings of these creatures, and their existence in the physical world (as opposed to the thunderbird who only lives in the spiritual world) is taken as a given. The tales say it lives in very deep water. Some tribes state that these animals follow a migratory path, with most sightings in BC occurring between October and April. This would make sense if we accept that it is a large species which requires an abundance of food as the surface water is coldest during this period and contains the highest concentration of small prey species. Marinebio.org explains why:

During the summer, the phytoplankton absorb most of the dissolved inorganic nutrients from the surface waters and are consumed by the zooplankton, decreasing the rate of photosynthesis. Vertical mixing ceases and phytoplankton, which remain in the upper layers, become nutrient-limited. The cycle starts all over in the fall when the surface water cools, churning the deeper, nutrient-rich waters into the depleted surface waters. Nutrients become available again and the phytoplankton blooms in great quantity during the spring after the intense winter mixing. Fall and summer are the least plentiful months due to the less active summer waters.

Basically, nutrients are brought to the surface with colder water in the winter, and phytoplankton follow. Zooplankton eat them, small fish eat them, big fish eat them – and Elton John explained the rest when he sang "that's the circle of life." A lot of big animals come to the surface from the deep in the winter for the feast.

To complicate things, other legends say Caddy is spotted most frequently when the waters are warm. Modern sightings (that I researched) tend to occur most during the October–April timeframe. I'm going with cold water sightings for the purposes of this chapter.

Let's then move on to what Caddy is *not* reported to be. Caddy is not reported to be a trans-dimensional being. Caddy is not reported to be able to teleport. Caddy cannot speak. Or fly. Caddy cannot breathe fire. Caddy is not a spirit animal or the ghost of a long-lost seaman. Caddy cannot communicate telepathically, lead minions of the deep, or raise the dead. Caddy is, by all reports, a run-of-the-mill sea creature. Mundane in all things other than size, shape, and, its lack of formal documentation.

The above bizarre statements are important, however. It's unfair to lump Caddy into the same category as ghosts, vampires, demons, and dimension-hopping bigfoots (as opposed to your standard giant, upright-walking, ape-man bigfoots). To believe in the possibility, even likelihood, of Caddy, you don't need to suspend disbelief. You don't need to bend the laws of physics, invoke the great unknowable spirit world, or create bizarre and impossibly unlikely biological adaptations. All you need to accept is that the ocean is extremely vast and we know very little about its inhabitants, particularly the deep sea dwellers.

Okay, so – assuming Caddy is a flesh-and-blood creature, why don't we have a live one, a body, or at least a good, clear photo? It's not like BC is Antarctica. Well, in fact, a lot of people have stories about capturing a live one, including Gary. Gary, of the Snuneymuxw People, told me that two of his mom's friends caught a young one. She saw it and told them they shouldn't touch it. They ignored her, but when the creature made a strange, loud cry they let it go as they were afraid it was calling to its mother. The Snuneymuxw revere the creature, and believe it is bad luck to catch one. Others have brought forward numerous "blobsquatches" that they claim to be the decomposing carcasses of Caddy. The most famous is known as the "Naden Harbor carcass."

A body of a creature was recovered from the stomach of a sperm whale in 1937 and photographed in Naden Harbor. No biologist has ever been able to positively ID the specimen in the photo. Some say it's indicative of a new species, others that it's a fetal baleen whale, others a basking shark – the truth is, we don't know and we won't ever know. I think the photo of the carcass is interesting, but without a DNA sample it has to stay in the "De Loy's Ape" category – at best unclear, at worst a purposeful hoax.

Bodies of large deep-sea marine animals are rarely recovered. Usually, they sink to the bottom before any person has the chance to see them, or float in the massive open ocean where no human is likely to ever cross their path before they either sink or are completely consumed by scavengers. The short of it is – we just don't often see a number of marine species, alive or dead.

If Caddy is a large marine species, it's likely somewhat migratory, as most known large marine species are – so why is it only spotted off North America's Pacific Coast? Glad you asked, voice in my head. The geologic structures of British Columbia's coast provide an ideal spot for sighting a large, deep-sea creature as the shore drops off dramatically to very deep water and the area is fairly well populated. Let's say these animals do exist. If they were to surface from the depths in most places where the ocean is 1,000-plus feet deep there would be no land within sight, and many of the places where land would be in sight are sparsely populated. British Columbia provides a good chance for a creature that normally stays deep below the ocean's surface to be seen by people.

There are more and more ships on the ocean, and more and more underwater surveillance, but, even so, the open ocean is a vast and unseen desert whose depths are the least explored part of our world. Before going down in the sub, we sent a remotely operated underwater vehicle (ROV) a few hundred feet down. We had agreed to film a promo reel for an ROV company in exchange for letting us use their tech. It was the most expensive ROV on the market, the most maneuverable, and the best equipped for truly deep dives. The water was calm at the surface, but there was a slight current about 100 feet down. Jim, the ROV "pilot," told us these were nearly ideal conditions.

We plopped the unthinkably expensive machine into the water and it started diving, with Jim guiding it. As it sank deeper and deeper, Jim started showing off its vast array of features – suction-powered collecting tubes, grasper hands capable of performing delicate tasks, and a multitude of lights of varying brightness and color. It swam forward and backwards and went up and down effortlessly in the water column, and clearly showed itself to be a useful tool for many underwater activities.

Its radar told us that it was approaching the bottom, and when it touched down it sent up a cloud of muck that took about five minutes to clear. Once it did, we started seeing fish, crabs, and garbage on the bottom. Jim turned the control over to me, and once I got the hang of it, I started to feel like I was playing the coolest videogame ever. I was approaching a large rock on the bottom about 15 minutes later when Jim suggested I raise up about 10 feet to clear it. I started to maneuver the ROV, but it suddenly jerked to a stop and wouldn't move at all. Jim took over and after 20 minutes of struggling was able to maneuver one of the cameras enough to see that the ROVs umbilical cord was caught on a piece of debris. Forty-five minutes later it was still caught, and 30 minutes after that we had to cut the $15,000 fiber-optic cable, tie it to a buoy, and leave it there for Jim to retrieve after donning his scuba gear. What I mean to say by telling this story is that, even with the best technology, just 500 feet below the surface is very hard to explore, and you only see what is directly in front of your cameras and lights.

I feel like I have set the stage – primed the pump, so to speak. Even the most closed-minded skeptic is now, I hope, at least open to the *possibility* that Caddy represents a new species – likely multiple species, actually. The descriptions vary so widely in many critical ways that it's very hard to talk about just one distinct animal when you talk about Caddy. For our purposes here let's assume that Caddy exists, is one distinct species, and for each type of animal I discuss that Caddy is an unknown/unidentified *type* of that animal. The reality is that many sightings are probably a combination of known animals, or possibly a combination of known and unknown animals – but again, when I say "reptile," I am saying, "What is the likelihood that Caddy (as a singular yet-to-be-discovered species) is a reptile?" Phew. Glad to get that out of the way. Now, with our newfound understanding and open-minded enthusiasm, let's look at some of the usual suspects.

## Surviving dinosaur

I address my feelings on living dinosaurs in the Mokele M'bembe book, but a slight rehash might be appropriate in case you haven't already purchased all of the books in the *On the Hunt* series. In short, there are no living dinosaurs. Not in swamps, on land, in lakes, or in the sea. None.[1] The idea that Caddy, Nessie, Champ, or any supposed water monster is a plesiosaur is based on outdated ideas of their biology, unclear sightings, and a lack of understanding about the true effects of the extinction event that wiped out the dinosaurs. A plesiosaur's anatomy wouldn't have allowed it to "swan" its neck out of the water in the way these cryptids are "sighted" as doing. People's minds often interpret the data they see in weird ways and find the closest match – a floating log can become a plesiosaur pretty easily. And the extinction event – K-PG, formerly K-T – was an effective kill event which wiped out approximately 75% of all multi-cellular life on Earth. The hardest-hit groups were large animals with high metabolisms – plesiosaurs fall into this category. This isn't to say that there isn't a large undiscovered animal in the waters off BC – I believe there is, in fact – but it is not a dinosaur.

## Reptile

For some reason, something about the "unknown reptile"

---

1 Of course I am aware of crocodiles, birds, horseshoe crabs, and other animals which have survived since the time of the dinosaurs, or evolved from them. When I say "there are no dinosaurs," I mean there are no living animals that would be at home in a Jurassic Park movie – "classic" dinosaurs from kids' books, in other words. Animals that your eight-year-old self would recognize as a dinosaur. Also – when I say "dinosaur" I mean it in the same way an eight-year-old would – a badass ancient animal. I know plesiosaurs and other animals that I mention in here are not dinosaurs, they are, in that instance, Mesozoic marine reptiles – don't @ me bro.

hypothesis *feels* wrong when you first consider it. This is, in fact, the fourth version of this chapter because I struggled so hard *against* the possibility that Caddy could be a reptile that I initially called it impossible in this section. But as I was writing, I kept coming up with more and more examples that show a large unknown reptile is, if not the most likely explanation for Caddy, at least a possibility. At a glance, a reptile of the size, shape, and behavior reported would seem to be completely unique in modern biology. But, much like the Mongolian Death Worm (another cryptid that I investigated), as outrageous as it sounds, there are examples of all of the traits in nature and precedents for the required adaptations. Arguing for or against the unknown reptile hypothesis presents some challenges – and not just because there is so much we don't know about the creature and so many conflicting reports, but because there is such a vast diversity of reptile species and so many incredible adaptations that show known examples of overcoming the hurdles that a species like Caddy would face.

In staying hidden from modern science but also just surviving in BC, a few of the obstacles that *any* animal meeting Caddy's description would seemingly need to overcome are: the temperature of the water it's found in; its size; its food source (which is related both to the size and temperature for reptiles); its habitat (presumed to be the deep ocean); and the lack of a carcass. That's a lot for one monster to contend with, but reptiles actually could overcome all of these, theoretically.

The temperature of the water seems like the first hurdle. Caddy lives in cold waters and is most often seen when the water is especially cold. When we think of reptiles we don't usually think of the cold – we think of animals basking in the sun, scurrying up palm trees, and lurking in tropical swamps. Hot environments, in other words. Even marine reptiles – snakes and turtles – make us think of white sand, clear blue water, and drinks with umbrellas in them. But not all reptiles live in warm climates. The largest snake den in the world is in central Canada, in fact, but those snakes den together in a hibernaculum all winter below the frostline as a survival strategy. Actually, all terrestrial reptiles in colder climates have a coping strategy for the winter/cold temperatures that involves a hibernation-type metabolic slow-down. Some burrow under ponds, some get below the frostline in the tangled underground maze of tree roots, some hide in decaying plant matter – none are active and moving around by the time Santa Claus comes to town. Marine environments are different, however.

Maintaining a reasonable body temperature to carry out metabolic processes is easy for reptiles; they just don't usually do it themselves. They rely on their environment to warm them and keep them that way. Their bodies will shut down if they get too cold as their various life functions (enzymes and whatnot) occur in a particular temperature range. If they are out of this range, the process cannot happen. An easily-illustrated example of this shutdown is digestion, which occurs at a pretty high temperature. If the body isn't warm enough, reptiles can't digest their food, and it can actually rot in their stomach, poisoning and killing them. This has been documented in large snakes and crocodilians that were either out of their normal habitat or got stuck in a cold snap after eating a big meal.

Some reptiles can control their internal body temperature, however. The leatherback turtle is remarkably adept at regulating its body temperature using muscle-generated heat and is found in British Columbian waters and even the Arctic Circle, which is some *seriously* cold water. Leatherbacks, which are the fastest-moving reptiles, spend less than 0.1% of their day resting. Crocodiles, on the flipside, spend about that much time active. They are exceptionally lethargic, with their massive size encouraging a more sedentary lifestyle. They need frequent rests to absorb the warming rays and digest their meals. If Caddy were a reptile, could it utilize a thermoregulation strategy more akin to a leatherback than a crocodile? It's possible. But the more active it is, the more likely we are to see it. If it's at the surface, we would more easily spot a fast-moving giant animal from humanity's vast array of shipping vessels, fishing boats, and cruise ships all over the world. If it's in the deep ocean, moving fast and covering huge distances, it's more likely to get caught in the thousands of miles of active, passive, and abandoned fishing nets. It's tough to think of a huge animal swimming as fast and as far as a leatherback and not occasionally coming up in a net, and as far as we know, in modern history, this has never happened. (The carcass seen in the famous Japanese fishing boat photos is a shark – sorry, that's science.)

Comparing croc and leatherback activity levels might come down to a difference in food sources. Leatherbacks eat jellyfish almost exclusively, which are not part of a very nutrient or fat-rich diet, and they have to eat a lot of them – up to their entire body weight each day – to sustain their metabolism. I've eaten quite a few jellyfish and really enjoy them (especially with some garlic and chili sauce), but even after a lot of them you don't get that "I want to unbutton my pants and start to fall asleep" feeling that comes from other animal-rich meals. Fatty meals seem to encourage longer digestion.

Leatherbacks are not gorging themselves on large fatty mammals or fish like crocs are. Any large reptile that eats meat or large fish needs extended periods of rest in a warm environment in order to digest – anacondas, pythons, crocodilians, Komodo dragons, etc. That amount of "heavy" food in their gut requires digestion time and high temperatures to accommodate it.

Could Caddy be eating jellyfish, like the leatherback? Or krill, like the basking shark? Maybe, but the description of its head, neck, and body would suggest otherwise, plus there are reports of them chasing salmon and seabirds. If we accept that the animal described has a long thin neck and horse/camel-like head, and we look at other animals with this body type, we see predators. Many marine dinosaurs show this body type and are all predatory: various pinnipeds (look at their skeletons, not their cute furry faces) – predators; various marine/wading birds – predators; various monitor lizards (again, look at their skeletal structures) – predators; and giraffes – leaf eaters – interesting, but not marine. In evolution's "use it or lose it" arms race, you don't develop a long, flexible neck and maneuverable head in a marine environment to catch krill or slow-moving jelly fish – you develop it to catch fast, hard-to-outmaneuver fish, birds, or mammals. The same can be said of a snake-shaped animal – they are all predators. Snakes, barracuda, eels, gar, arawana, and pike all twist, turn, dart, and outmaneuver their prey. That body shape is not for filter feeding or eating veggies, and jellyfish are essentially one step above veggies in terms of maneuverability and difficulty to catch.

Could they be eating seals? This is another tough sell, in my opinion. For one thing, we know a pretty good amount about all of the world's seal populations. We know where they breed, migrate, etc., and what hunts them because of this. Most animals that hunt seals gather where the seals are the most vulnerable – their breeding grounds. White sharks, orcas, polar bears – all are found where the seals are found. We also have some of the best footage of these animals while hunting/eating seals because these attacks happen at the surface. If a large animal like Caddy was going to go undocumented for so long, I can't imagine them flipping seals into their mouths like a hibachi chef with a teriyaki shrimp in places where the world's photographers converge to get that perfect shot of a baby seal's puppy eyes reflected in a stone-cold killer's stare. Unless one proposes an unknown species of seal that breeds in an unknown location, of course, but that gets us on the wrong side of Occam's Razor pretty quickly.

There's also the size to contend with – the largest known extant reptile is the saltwater crocodile which can reach lengths of well over 20 feet. That's a far cry from the sixty-foot estimates some eyewitnesses have given Caddy, but I think that huge is huge. A 20-foot crocodile is huge, and it's an accepted fact that eyewitnesses are bad judges of size. So, I will give hardcore believers the benefit of saying the size of a croc exceeds the size requirements for Caddy. So, what's the issue? Size seems to be accounted for – both size and shape, in fact, which are a boon for many marine animals with the tube-like shape providing insulation and decreasing surface area, thereby adding efficiency in thermoregulation, as shown above. The issue is, as discussed, that crocs need the warmth of their environment to digest, and other meat eaters like sharks generate the same muscle-generated warmth that a leatherback benefits from. So, for Caddy to be a large reptile it would have to either bask in the sun like a croc or utilize muscle-generated warmth.

Caddy is often described as incredibly fast. Some alleged footage shows ocean spray from the impressive speed of the supposed creature. Some reports describe it covering great distances in short amounts of time, and these are sometimes attributed to its size rather than its speed. "I saw a hump, then I saw another hump 30 feet away not two seconds later" – that sort of thing. Could this be an indication of speed? Sure. Might Caddy rival the leatherback as the fastest reptile in the sea? It might. A couple of eyewitnesses I spoke with talked about an animal that could easily outstrip their motor boats, fishing boats, or other crafts. Those that saw it from the land say they'd never seen another marine animal move that fast. So, this speed could potentially produce muscle heat to counteract the cold water, just as leatherbacks do, or it could really be 60 feet long and people are only seeing small parts of it. Speed seems more likely than size, in my opinion, but once again this increases the likelihood of us seeing it.

Gigantothermy (sometimes called ectothermic homeother-my) could also come into play to explain how an animal meeting Caddy's description could be a reptile in cold water. Gigantothermy says that large ectothermic (cold-blooded) animals can maintain a constant, relatively high body temperature more easily than smaller animals due to their surface area to volume ratio. The larger the animal, the smaller (proportionally) the portion of it exposed to the environment. This concept is used to explain how massive marine dinosaurs like ichthyosaurs and mosasaurs maintained the high body temperatures required to digest their large prey. So, Caddy's anatomy would suggest that it eats larger, faster prey, and we have precedence for this in cold-water ectotherms. We also have the largest turtle in the world living in freezing water. I have to say, temperature of the water, potential size of the animal, and potential food source, do not rule out "reptile" for Caddy's ID.

All crocodilians spend the majority of their time on land or in the shallows. Yes, they occasionally make a long-distance journey, but they rarely muscle through it, instead relying on currents to carry them the distance while they exert minimal effort. An open-ocean free-swimming croc seems a far cry from the crocodilians we know of. Could one have adapted to a more aquatic life? Yes, a short leap from semi to primarily aquatic seems plausible, but (and here is where we get to the next massive hurdle), it would still be an air-breathing reptile. It wouldn't live in the depths; it would be a surface dweller.

There were some pretty impressive pre-crocodilian species (called crocodilliforms) millions of years ago. Metriorhynchus was essentially a fully marine croc, but would have lived in warm seas close to the surface. Nothing is known about how it reproduced, but it's possible it had live births, like a sauropod. There was also the slightly more contemporary Stomatosuchus – a toothless croc with a pelican-like throat pouch, which was primarily (if not entirely) aquatic/marine. Once again, warm water, and close to the surface.

A reptile would have to come to the surface to breathe, and

this would increase the likelihood of spotting it anywhere in its range. If Caddy were a reptile, it would negate the "British Columbia opens to deep water close to shore" argument as an explanation for sightings. I believe of all the traits that make Caddy believable, living in deep water is the key selling point, and a reptile would not spend the majority of its life in deep water, would it? The "large animals yet to be discovered in the ocean" scientists quoted above all cite "deep water" as the most likely refuge for unique undiscovered species. While not entirely out of the question, an unknown, 15-foot air-breather is a tougher sell. I don't want to revisit dinosaurs, but even ancient reptiles breathed air, and did not live in the deep sea.

Some freshwater turtles can stay submerged for months at a time. The musk turtle absorbs oxygen through a highly specialized tongue during these underwater sojourns. The Fitzroy river turtle in Australia can stay submerged almost indefinitely and absorbs oxygen through its cloaca. The cloaca is a multipurpose hole shared by the digestive, reproductive, and, in some cases, respiratory systems. It's position, however, gives no doubt that it is, in fact, a fancy name for a butthole. The Fitzroy river turtle breathes through its butt. "Fitzroy" is far too elegant a name for an animal that respires in such an undignified way. Think of poor Fitzroy's breath. Interestingly, the sea cucumber also respires using its cloaca, and a multitude of marine creatures like tiny fish and crabs often live their presumably disgusting lives inside the sea cucumber's butthole. That is an impressive orifice, if ever I've seen one. They emerge from the anus of the echinoderm each night to forage for food. Why at night? Because they literally live in an asshole and they're embarrassed, and don't want the other fish and crabs to point at them and shout, "Hey everybody! Look, there's Marc, he lives inside the sea cucumber's anus!"

Anyway, none of these turtles are very active while utilizing cloacal respiration. Most stay underwater for the winter months in a slowed metabolism/hibernation mode, and the Fitzroy barely moves at all while submerged. It stays put just trying to look like a rock, and succeeding – just a rock that breathes through its butthole. No marine reptiles have been shown to use this particular respiration strategy, and the longest any active marine turtle can stay submerged is the leatherback at about two hours (sea turtles sleep and some can even semi-hibernate for much longer, but, again – "active" is the key word here).

This does show that this adaptation exists in aquatic reptiles, however, and we can't say there *isn't* a marine species that has an even more impressive butthole than the Fitzroy. That came out wrong, what I meant was, it's possible that some reptiles can do all kinds of things with their buttholes. I'll stop now, but it is scientifically plausible to say a cloacal-breathing strategy could have evolved in a marine reptile, particularly a turtle with their weird water-land-water-land-water proposed evolution. Google it.

Anyway, back to ass breathing – could it be that Caddy employs a strategy like the Fitzroy turtle during periods of lower activity, resting on the bottom for long periods then rising to the surface and air-breathing during energetic bursts, like when hunting for salmon, snapping at gulls, and messing with drunk college kids who totally had permission to take Dad's boat, broseph? It's possible, theoretically – but unlikely when you look at other marine species. The deep sea is a place of energy conservation, where nearly all life appears to employ a "lie and wait" strategy for hunting. There isn't an adaptive pressure to produce a *reptile* that lives both in the depths (most of the time) and at the surface (to hunt) due to the overwhelming difficulties the animal would face, and there are much easier ways to overcome them. At first glance, this isn't intuitive. The surface certainly has a lot more prey available, and the depths provide an ideal "sit back and digest in safety" location. A lot of marine species head up to the surface at night to feed then sink back down to the deep as the sun rises. These are purely aquatic species, however, not air breathers, and they don't have the other anatomical difficulties we've discussed for marine reptiles. Remember, evolution is a path of least resistance process. If the animal survives to pass on its traits, its traits survive as well. Did the animal find food? Excellent. You live and reproduce. Was there more food elsewhere? Yup, but that doesn't matter – it was harder to get to, and the food this animal found kept it alive just as well.

Well, some large reptiles, particularly constrictors, also hunt and digest in different environs. They head onto land to catch a big meal, then slink to the safety of a muddy river to rest undisturbed while they digest for a couple of months, camouflaged in the murky water. But that's in the Tropics – remember, reptiles in cold water generate the necessary muscle-generated heat to stay alive by being very active. A reptile at rest down below 1,000 feet would be at a fairly constant 2–4°C – far too low to maintain its metabolic processes. If we go with the "hunt at the surface, digest in the deep" theory, we are left with even more of a problem in that digestion is one of the processes that occurs at a higher temperature for reptiles. It just doesn't make sense for that to develop. What about hunt in the deep and digest up top, in the warm sun? Again, why seek out a food source in the deep ocean? What adaptive pressure would there be for a reptile to dive deeper and deeper when there is ample food available at the surface? I have to admit that walruses and gray whales do this, but we then once again struggle to answer the question of "why haven't we seen one?" Could either of these scenarios happen? Yes, but why would they? I'm exhausted just thinking about the myriad of adaptations such an animal would need.

There is reproduction to consider as well. Most marine reptiles (and all of the large ones) lay eggs on land. No report I've ever heard has described a Caddy on a beach laying eggs.

Maybe there is an undiscovered Monster Island in the Pacific where Caddys (is the plural Caddies? Or is that strictly for golf assistants?) are crawling up on shore to deposit their eggs and baby hatchlings are engaging in epic battles with seabirds, but I think we'd have seen "Caddy Beach" by now if it exists. (It does raise a question, though – why don't we don't we have a "Caddy Beach" movie yet?) They could lay eggs, like a squid, but no marine reptile does this so I'll say it's unlikely.

They could give birth to live young, called "ovoviparous" in reptiles where the eggs incubate and hatch inside the mother, who then appears to birth the babies. Only about 20% of terrestrial reptiles do this, but as for marine – nearly all sea snakes do. Interestingly, it's theorized that colder temperatures push reptiles and amphibians to give live birth rather than lay eggs. The colder the temperature, the longer the female generally holds the eggs until, in some cases, she holds them right until they hatch and she gives "live" birth. This is how it is believed viviparity (live birth) evolved in reptiles and their ancestors. Some skink species spread over multiple climates still show this variation – individuals in the coldest regions give "live birth" while those in warmer regions lay eggs. It's theorized that the transition from eggs to "live birth" isn't a very difficult one for evolution to tackle, and in fact might be an easy-to-make adaptation rather than a slow and gradual change.

This fact does push the "Caddy is a reptile" argument forward a bit. If Caddy were a reptile, there is an argument to be made for a "live birth" scenario, but baby Caddy would likely not be as adept at holding its breath as adult Caddy, and would therefore need to spend more time at the surface. This is anecdotally true in all marine air-breathers. Also, the young would not benefit from gigantism, and would not have a blubber layer. They would have to be born in warm water, yet many reports describe a "smaller," typically thought to be a "young," Caddy in BC. I would postulate these are cases of mistaken identity.

There is a chance that people are seeing the head or body of a known or unknown reptile along with a pod of dolphins or other marine animals (the dolphins accounting for the humps), but I doubt it. I don't think there is a completely unique unknown reptile species in BC. Might we find a new subspecies of sea turtle using genetic testing? Sure, but I would bet money that to the untrained eye it looks a lot like other sea turtles. Maybe a new species of sea snake? Yes, but again it will likely look like other sea snakes, be fairly small, live in warm waters, and swim with a side-to-side motion, not up-and-down like a marine mammal or how Caddy is reported to move. I think it is likely that some Caddy sightings are a leatherback or other large turtle with various marine life around them. They aren't frequently seen in British Columbia, and it's likely that even a seasoned fisherman could go their entire life without encountering one. If you just saw a leatherback's head as it popped up for air and there was a pod of dolphins or other marine life nearby, I could see it being mistaken for a massive sea serpent. I could even see some sightings of an out-of-place crocodilian accounting for it. Alligators are not native to my hometown of Boston, but that doesn't stop people finding a couple every summer in the local waterways. People release pets, animals get blown to strange locations in storms, currents shift and bring animals to places where they are foreign – it happens, all the time, and likely leads to some very confused eyewitnesses. I can't blame them. A 2,000-pound, nine-foot leatherback with a massive fat head and eight foot flippers *is* a sea monster. Take the fact that it follows jellyfish, and, as shown above, jellyfish are most populous off of BC during the times when Caddy is most frequently spotted, and you have a great recipe for misidentification.

It could also be a huge group of known species. Sea snakes do show up sometimes in massive numbers. In 1932, a ship in Malaysia reported a sighting of an insane gathering of Stokes sea snakes. The report says there was a line 10 feet wide and over 60 miles long of writhing sea snakes. This outrageous number of snakes has never been seen again – maybe it was a once in a lifetime party. Maybe the snake version of the Beatles got back together and they all showed up to see them – we may never know – but this species is often spotted in groups numbering thousands of individuals. The yellow-belly is the most pelagic (living in the open ocean) and widespread species of sea snake, and is also known to gather in the thousands. It is possible that one of these huge groups was transported from their normal habitat in Baja, California, to the freezing waters of BC before it knew what had happened. I think it's entirely possible that people seeing it from a distance could think it was one massive sea serpent. It could happen on a freak tide every hundred years, or something, and then all of the snakes freeze to death in a couple of days, or are eaten by excited seals or other marine life. I don't know, but I think it's more likely than an unknown reptile. (Incidentally, the Anaconda mating ball is, I believe, most likely the explanation for "cobra grande" in much the same way.)

So, what do we have for our reptile hypothesis?

Cold water – it could generate body heat with fast swimming like a leatherback, but this is unlikely because that would increase the likelihood of seeing it.

Food source – it could eat jellyfish like a leatherback, but this is unlikely based on its described anatomy. It could eat seals, but this is unlikely based on our not seeing one near seal-pupping grounds. It could eat fish, but digestion in cold temperatures is a challenge without fast movement.

Air breathing – it could breathe through its butt like a turtle, but this is unlikely as it doesn't give enough oxygen for an energetic reptile, and is more of a "lie and wait" method for survival, which is not how Caddy is described. It's also not a good strategy for a large animal that needs significantly more oxygen to support its bulk and needs to release a lot more carbon dioxide. Could it lay low in the depths, employing butt breathing, then come to the surface for big gulps of air? Yes, it could, but why would it? It just doesn't fit that an animal would develop all of the necessary adaptations for life under the extreme pressure and coldness of the deep *and* the dangers of being at the surface. It doesn't make sense from an evolutionary perspective – what would drive those adaptations that couldn't allow for survival in a much easier way? Presumably, this is also ruled out because a young animal wouldn't be able to do this due to heat-loss/increased surface area.

Reproduction – it could give birth to live young, but the baby would be unlikely to survive undetected as it would need more food and warm waters, and to surface more frequently.

(For further reading, LeBlond and Bousfield make a compelling argument for Caddy being a reptile, but Aaron Bauer, Anthony Russell, and Darren Naish do a great job of refuting these claims.)

## Amphibian

I almost finished this section without mentioning amphibians. It seems ridiculous to even bring this group up, and it is rarely mentioned as a serious possibility for Caddy. After all, there are no known marine frogs, salamanders, caellians, sirens, etc., right? It *should* be at least slightly easier to make the case that modern amphibians are very adapted to a freshwater environment, and their permeable skin would not make a good barrier against a salt-rich marine ecosystem. They would die from dehydration and ion imbalance pretty quickly, right? They fare even more poorly in cold temperatures than a reptile, right? Well, maybe not, it turns out.

I can remember spending hours every day searching for animals in the creek near my childhood home (pronounced "crick" in one of the last vestiges of the upstate NY accent I've retained) while my mom watched, ensuring I didn't drown or get distracted and wander off – equally likely scenarios when I was immersed in observations of the natural world. I found minnows, Dobson-fly larvae, pollywogs, frog's eggs, toads, crayfish, snakes, and much more in its waters and on the muddy banks. I filled aquariums with these creatures and, adhering to my mother's rules for once, would release them back into the water the next day and lug home a new batch to observe for the night. I put samples of the water under my microscope and discovered an entirely different world living in that creek.

These observations didn't stop when the weather turned cold. Once the water froze over, I simply donned some ice skates and, while my friends and family skated, cleared a spot on the ice to create a viewing window, then lay on my stomach and searched for the animals I'd observed in the preceding months. I was rewarded with young bass, trout, the occasional crayfish, and once, under possibly a foot of ice, in the crystal-clear and frigid water, I saw a frog swim by as if I was looking at it through the glass of an aquarium. That image has stayed with me, and reminds me that animals don't always act like you think they are supposed to.

There are frogs in the French Alps, a sub-species of the common European frog, that are famous for emerging and mating in the snows of early spring. The snow there doesn't melt until June, so there is a very short window to mate, lay eggs, and allow the juveniles a chance to grow a bit before the freezing temperatures return. The cold weather has pushed a few other adaptations. These frogs grow much larger than others in their species in warmer climates and live more than double the average lifespan of the rest of their compatriots – 12 years on average, compared to five for their lowland brethren. They also lay eggs which are around 30% larger than the norm for their species, have developed a resistance to UV radiation (important at an elevation of over 6,000 feet), and, interestingly, get into position to mate before hibernating so as to not lose any time once the short spring arrives. This means the males find a female to latch onto and hold for the entire winter – a wintering strategy I would also employ, if my wife were into it.

There *are* other cold and even brackish water amphibians, and they're all big. The BC giant pacific salamander survives in very cold water and has a tendency toward neonatancy – a trait where the species in question stays a perpetual juvenile (like human males). The tiger salamander (also in British Columbia) lives in saline lakes and also exhibits neonatancy. It eats virtually any living thing that fits in its mouth, and reproduces at the bottom of the deep lakes.

Crab-eating frogs in Asia hunt in the ocean. The hellbender salamander lives in cold water in America's heartland and is so adapt at absorbing oxygen from the fast-flowing streams it inhabits that it never has to surface to breathe, a trait it shares with the largest salamanders on Earth. The giant Japanese and Chinese salamanders reach lengths of over five feet and live in very cold water. They also live a long life of 200-plus years down in their rocky streams, and are rarely ever seen.

It appears that cold water pushes towards a longer life generally, not just for amphibians. One of the longest-living species is the Antarctic clam, an individual of which was found to be over 600 years old. Cold temperatures also push towards giving live birth, as stated earlier. Salinity may push towards mating at greater depths as it is saltier at the surface, so would push a salt-sensitive species to potentially deposit spermatophores at the bottom, like a tiger salamander does. Cold temperatures can also push amphibians towards neonatancy like the Mexican Taylor's salamander, which also lives in very cold saline environments, and is so adept at living in saltwater that it appears to be dependent on it. (Did you notice all of the examples from British Columbia earlier? BC has a history of weird amphibians!)

But wait, there's more – what about amphibian shape? Amphiuma are a species of snake-like salamanders that grow to about 4 feet and are fully aquatic. They are also the only salamander that can whistle (which Caddy is sometimes said to do). Caecillians are a very poorly understood group of amphibians that are snake-like in appearance, almost all giving live birth, and at least one species of which increases its weight about tenfold a week after giving birth by growing an extremely fatty, nutrient-rich outer layer of skin and letting their babies eat it. Baja worm lizards are bizarre little dragon-looking things with tiny weird arms and hands. All salamanders exhibiting neonatancy also have knobby protrusions on top of their heads, like Caddy, which are their external gills (like an axolotl).

Pacific giant salamanders are the largest terrestrial salamander in the Americas and are one of the largest terrestrial salamanders in the world. Adults of this species may exhibit neonatancy and retain gills to live a more aquatic lifestyle, as mentioned above, or may metamorphose completely and live terrestrially. Gilled, aquatic adults are common in more coastal populations and those of, you guessed it, British Columbia. When you witness the size and big puppy-dog eyes of this salamander, you can see how they might be an explanation for "baby Caddys" caught by people. They really do fit the description very well.

In general, cold water seems to change many species, giving them a variety of odd traits. Polar "embryo gigantism" appears to be considerably more widespread than adult gigantism, for example. If there is a tendency towards neonatancy in colder water, is it that great a leap to expect to see a giant, neonate in cold water? In an article for the *Journal of Experimental Biology* in 2012, Moran and Woods explain it like this:

The extreme, constant cold of polar marine environments has been implicated in many unusual traits, including gigantism, extreme stenothermality, freeze tolerance and changes in oxygen carrying and storage capacity. In general, these traits are interpreted as adaptive, though we do not always understand the underlying factors that have driven their evolution, or whether some may be "disaptations" allowed by polar conditions.

Finally, before leaving amphibians as a big "maybe," there were marine amphibians – huge ones – in ancient times. Again, surviving dinosaurs are a tough sell, and I'm not trying to be the salesman, I'm just saying – it's possible to have an amphibian that lives in cold, salty water. It's actually not as easy to write off as most scientists would like it to be, especially when you start seeing that cold, salty water pushes a species to live longer, get larger, give live birth, grow faster, and spend more time at the bottom of the body of water.

## Shark

I'm trying not to repeat myself, so I will say that many of the arguments covered in reptiles and amphibians above also apply to the other animal types. I'll try to focus on the specific examples of unusual species of each group which demonstrate that a Caddy-like creature in the animal group could overcome the challenges presented by the group's anatomical features.

When presented with the word "shark" most people think of *Jaws*. This makes sense as that movie, more than anything else, gave us a physical manifestation of all that we fear about the ocean. Its main antagonist was silent, massive, mysterious, and deadly. It also had awesome music. *Jaws* was terrifying. Sharks are terrifying. But *Jaws* did many disservices to these marvelous creatures; aside from inspiring thousands of well-intentioned and completely ineffective shark massacres, it also gave sharks a physical image and set a standard that few sharks can live up to. Like male models. Not all of us can have six-pack abs, okay? We get it, you have perfect cheekbones and 2% body fat; put a shirt on, please, you're causing a scene in the mall and I'm just trying to buy a pair of cargo shorts. It feels like I'm drinking cheap cologne every time I take a breath in here.

As far as behaviors go, most of us normal men will never play a shirtless game of rugby with our bros, and no sharks act like the one in *Jaws*. The vast majority of species have never killed a man and certainly have never actively hunted a specific person (unlike male models). Many don't eat meat at all, in fact. The largest of all sharks, the 40-foot whale shark, feeds much like it's even larger namesake the baleen whale. The smallest, the dwarf lanternshark, maxes out at around eight inches and glows in the dark. There are other species displaying virtually every trait in between: sharks that take almost perfectly round bites out of giant prey; pink, red, black, and silver sharks; sharks with bizarre, alien-looking flat heads, or massively long, spiked "saw" noses; sharks that use farts to attain the right buoyancy; sharks that look like a throw rug, a leatherback turtle, a giant eel, or even thin, delicate corals – absolutely, guy, we've got 'em all here on Earth. Sharks are remarkably diverse and weird. Just Google image search "frilled shark" and "ghost shark" to get an idea.

Sharks live in the ocean and freshwater rivers and estuaries, and some of the warmest as well as the coldest on Earth. Sharks eat fish, seals, other sharks, turtles, cars, people, dogs, dolphins, whales, plankton, and basically anything else in the water. There is one captive nurse shark who has even decided to go vegetarian. Sharks are among the slowest non-sedentary and fastest swimming animals in the ocean. What I'm trying to say is – sharks are diverse.

Sharks are also notoriously hard to study, and even to find. Two new species of saw-sharks were discovered in March of 2020. We didn't even know where great whites breed and give birth until none other than Harry Marshall from Icon Films uncovered the necessary evidence in 2013. (Seriously, why isn't there a book about this guy?) Most marine biologists agree that some shark species are likely to go extinct before we even have a proper scientific name for them.

So could a shark look like Caddy? Yes, to some degree it could. The concept of convergent evolution says that unrelated animals who share the same niche will evolve to look like one another based on environmental drivers and natural selection. Think skates and flounder, thylacine and wolf, echidna and hedgehog, tegus and monitors, or sawfish and sawshark. Could a deep-water shark look more like a deep-water eel? Yes. In fact, one does – the frilled shark.

Could a shark have evolved to look like a plesiosaur? Sure it could, but it probably didn't. The plesiosaur shape was really good for very warm, nutrient and oxygen-rich seas with abundant life. This is the opposite of how we'd describe the deep sea. The plesiosaurs died out millions of years ago – as did all of the related species that looked like them – and no other animals have since been found with that shape. This tells us that there are other more efficient shapes for surviving in today's environments. The stock shark ancestor's shape was fairly tubular, robust, and streamlined – the frilled shark isn't *that* divergent from this model. As distinct as shark species look from each other, and as diverse as their behaviors and food sources are, their basic biology is remarkably similar. In order to appear Caddy-like, a shark would have to undergo a dramatic change in not just its form but also the function of many of its major biological systems. Does this happen in nature? Absolutely, but there is always an environmental pressure, and based on what we know about the plesiosaur and convergent evolution, the pressure doesn't exist to create an animal that looks this way.

Could a shark look more serpentine? Now we're talking! Yes, based on available evidence, the serpentine shape is a good one for many marine species and fits with shark biology. While the frilled shark is the most snake-like one we know of, there is no reason to think there couldn't be another shark out there that's even more serpentine. It's also entirely possible that many of the Caddy sightings are frilled sharks.

The sleeper shark, also called the Greenland shark, is fairly long and tubular (in the Teenage Mutant Ninja Turtles meaning of the word, as well as being literally tube-like). They are a great comparison also because they live in very deep, very cold water. Because of this, though, they also live in a near-perpetual state of dormancy. They are so slow moving in their frigid waters that people call them "sleeper" because they appear to be asleep. This can give us a glimpse at how a shark's biology could adapt to life in very deep, very cold water. With what we know about sleeper sharks, it would be very unlikely that another shark living in the same conditions would be extremely active and fast moving as Caddy is described, right? Makos, as the fastest shark, and sleepers, as the slowest, are both sharks and show us the incredible diversity of sharks and what the stock "shark" is capable of evolving into. But they each evolved under vastly different conditions and are each suited to vastly different environments. It would be highly unlikely that a mako and sleeper would evolve under the same conditions unless there was a new niche to fill. And yet, it turns out there is. It's actually not highly unlikely at all, once you think about it.

Hummingbirds and ostriches are two birds that evolved in the same area, under the same conditions, and that couldn't be more different. When animals speciate under the same conditions, it's a poorly understood aspect of evolution called "adaptive radiation." Look at the Lake Victoria cichlids. In a very short time, one stock "cichlid" species became about 500 distinct species – same lake, same driving forces, etc. What happened was new niches opened up, and the adaptive "cichlid" form could mold itself to exploit these niches, especially in terms of feeding adaptations. What we don't know is when these small variations in morphology led to a new species. Why would the cichlid with smaller lips adapt for eating algae, for instance, stop mating with the cichlids with slightly larger lips who eat parasites? At what point does that happen?

Anyway, back to sharks. Imagine you are a deep-water shark. Most food sources are slow, so you don't have to be fast and evolve to be very slow along with having glycoprotein anti-freeze and a kind of permanent half-sleepy slowed metabolism (like your stoner roommate), as well as a blubber layer, and stay a happy, sleepy, stoner shark.

Conversely, there are fast deep-sea squid, and who's going to eat them? Your cousin, the imaginary fast deep-water shark. This shark develops homeothermic muscle-generated heat like a mako and white shark, and chases the other fast animals like squid and even other sharks, and occasionally sealions and other deep divers. They also get a blubber layer and grow longer and more tubular, decreasing their surface area, live for a long time, get much larger, and migrate far and wide. Occasionally, they find themselves a little too far up in the water column, even breaching the surface once in a while, where they see the horrible two-legged things that live up there before flopping a few times and heading back down to their deep-sea home. Boom. Caddy. Maybe?

## Bony Fish

Bony fish live everywhere wet – fresh water, acidic water, hot water, below freezing water, on wet land (for days at a time in some cases), incredibly saline water (concentrated salt pools in mudflats), the deepest oceanic trenches, and the shallowest puddles. They are the largest and most diverse extant class of vertebrates with over 28,000 species. They range in size and shape from the dwarf pygmy goby (15 mm) to the ocean sunfish (over 5,000 pounds) and the bizarrely alien-looking deep-sea angler fish and the massive 60-foot-long oarfish. They have some of the most fantastic biological adaptations and a seemingly endless variety of "weird."

It's far from impossible to imagine a bony fish meeting Caddy's description. Strangely, the feature that most scientists point to in order to "prove" that Caddy cannot be a bony fish is its reported horizontal tail fluke for making "up and down" oscillations – like a manatee's tail. Only mammals have this horizontal tail fluke, and all known bony fish have vertical tails for "side-to-side" swimming motions. So says science, and it's not wrong. But it's not exactly right, either. Flatfish (flounder) exhibit a horizontal tail. They go through an extreme metamorphosis which eventually leads to the "bottom" of the fish actually being one of their sides, and the eye from that side migrating to the top, leaving both eyes on one side of the fish. It serves to give them the appearance of flapping their back fin "up and down," but anatomically this is still "side to side." I'm not claiming that Caddy has a similar morphological adaptation with its tail, I'm just saying it's not impossible for a bony fish to show up-and-down tail movements rather than side-to-side.

Onto the weird fish! This will be less a "Caddy *could* be a bony fish" and more a "of course Caddy could be a bony fish – look at all of these weird adaptations/morphological features!"

The opah – the moonfish – is a warm-blooded fish. It regulates its own body temperature, allowing it to survive in very cold deep water. Like the leatherback, it generates a lot of the body heat it needs from muscle movement.

The heaviest fish in the world is the mola-mola, or ocean sunfish. Again, like the leatherback, it eats almost exclusively jellyfish and is found in very cold water, including British Columbia. It is sometimes called the head fish as it looks like a giant, disembodied head. If you've never seen one – Google it. They are weird.

The oscillated icefish looks like a bird and a snake had an ugly baby. It inhabits Antarctic waters, which are often below freezing. What really separates it from the pack is its transparent blood, due to its lacking hemoglobin. It turns out that, at extremely cold temperatures, oxygen dissolves more easily into plasma. No one has any idea how it evolved this feature as it appears unique to the bony fish.

Stimpson's goby climbs very high waterfalls in Hawaii using its mouth. It undergoes an extreme metamorphosis with a sucker adaptation over the course of two days before its journey. That's right – it changes various features of its head pretty drastically in under 48 hours. Fish are weird.

The lancetfish looks like a dragon. An actual dragon. It seems more lizard than fish. We know very little about it other than it appears to live just about everywhere (including British Columbia), grows to almost 7 feet long, has been caught at nearly every depth up to 6,000 feet below the surface, is a voracious predator and cannibal, and appears to be a fast swimmer. Oh, and its meat is described as "watery and gelatinous," so if that's your thing, then lancetfish – it's what's for dinner. You weirdo.

The candiru is an Amazonian species most famous for swimming up the urethrae of very unfortunate swimmers. It follows the ammonia trail of urine, mistaking it for the ammonia released by fish, and tries to reach its preferred home of large fish's gills but occasionally ends up living inside a vertebrate's penis. This is usually a hippo, but sometimes a person, whose chances for a happy life after the fish takes up residence are not nearly as good as the well-endowed hippo. What does this have to do with Caddy? Nothing! But how could I not mention this in a chapter about weird fish?

The climbing perch, scourge of conservation groups everywhere, can survive out of water for up to six days, and inflates its body to suffocate would-be predators, lodging in their throats as they try to swallow the invasive species.

The various species of flying fish have adapted to, well, fly – "glide" is technically more correct, but for all intents and purposes it's flying. They can leap into the air for 45 seconds in a single bound, have been seen gaining 20 vertical feet out of the water and a distance of 1,300 feet in a single leap, traveling more than 70 miles per hour. That's flying in my book.

Hagfish are not bony fish, and neither are lampreys, but this seems like the best place to include them. They appear eel-like, but in truth are vastly different from eels. Lampreys have a modified mouth (they are jawless) which allows them to cling to and cut little holes out of fish or anything else swimming by. Evolutionarily, they are in a class all of their own. Hagfish are also jawless, but are even weirder than lampreys. They are mostly scavengers and are one of the very few animals that purposely tie themselves in knots. They get a mouthful of rotting fish, then, to get some purchase and tear a chunk off, wrap their body around their head and pull their head through. They also secrete copious amounts of slime – in fact, one hagfish can turn five gallons of water into milky, fibrous, slime in about two seconds. This can confuse, suffocate, or just gross out any predator. Both "fish" are found in BC.

In May 2015 it was reported that a giant 20-foot conger eel had been caught off the British coast. The story ran with an image of the monster hanging off the side of a dock. This goliath beast certainly solidified the belief that the species could be the culprit behind many "sea serpent" sightings. While this individual turned out to be a hoax, huge conger eels have been caught in the past. No known species live in British Columbia, however.

The oarfish is commonly heralded as the answer to most sea serpent sightings. It does seem to fit the bill pretty nicely. They have been found in nearly all of the world's oceans and yet are rarely seen (alive or dead), they reach mammoth sizes (some reports have them up to 60 feet long, but, realistically there are believable reports at nearly 40 feet and verifiable measurements of nearly 30), they are bizarre and snake-like in appearance, and we know very little about them. A live one swimming with a person was filmed in 2015. Amazingly, the person was the greatest host on TV, Jeremy Wade, and the filming was for an episode of *River Monsters*, another Icon Films production. It is some of the most surreal footage you've ever seen. This bizarre animal swims upright in the water column, but, when dying, has been known to surface and "flap" its massive body, creating a very sea serpent-like motion.

In general, I think I've shown that bony fish check all of the boxes needed for a Caddy-like creature. Add to this the concept of abyssal gigantism – animals living in the deep ocean tend to be much larger than their shallow-water counterparts – and polar gigantism – animals in colder water also tend to be larger than their warmer water counterparts – and you have a great argument for a large, pretty weird, deep-water, cold-water creature.

## Cetacean

Whales and dolphins check many of the boxes for a Caddy-like creature. Compared to some of the groups above, they have the added bonus of size. The blue whale is the largest animal to have ever existed. There were ancient whales that were more "Caddy shaped" (think basilosaurus), although we have no reason to think they could have survived. Although whales are mammals, and thus breath air, they are still very mysterious, and new species are still being discovered.

Beaked whales in particular are a tricky group. They are very deep divers and rarely seen. Cuvier's beaked whale dives over two miles deep, stays under for over two hours at a time, and barely breaks the surface to gulp some air before heading down to the depths again. It feeds almost exclusively on deep-sea squid and fish. Although it's the most common and far distributed beaked whale, it's nearly impossible to study. This whale damages the "Caddy can't be an air-breather" argument.

Many whale species are very migratory, as Caddy is reported to be. Whales also give birth to live young at sea, meaning the "Island of Caddy babies" doesn't have to exist. Whales also have the mammalian horizontal fluke mentioned above, which Caddy is said to possess. Whales are extremely intelligent, long lived, and shy – demonstrating avoidance behaviors rather than contacting humans. Toothed whales (like orcas) are also notorious for being aggressive predators.

There's also the "this sounds like a joke but holy shit that's actually possible" issue of a whale's penis. As previously mentioned, up to 16 feet long, rarely ever seen by people (except people with *very* niche interests I'm guessing), and some whales mate by going up to the surface and rolling onto their backs, extending their penises straight up in the air before rolling and diving to where a female is waiting. While at the surface, well, gravity tends to take over and make the whale's impressive member, sort of flop down a bit appearing to be a long neck with an odd shaped head. I'm not saying this accounts for a large number of sea serpent sightings, but, I think your buddies might be more interested in hearing about the time you saw a sea serpent versus the time you saw a whale's junk in the distance. I also have to think that the average person would not know what a whale's penis looks like out of the water, particularly in the days before the internet, and if you happened to be out on a boat at the right time and saw a 16-foot phallus appearing out of nowhere, then disappearing a few seconds later, your first thought probably would not be whale porn, I hope. It seems that there is an argument to be made for Caddy being a cetacean – or maybe part of a cetacean.

# Pinniped

The wonderfully brilliant and open-minded British vertebrate paleontologist and writer Dr. Darren Naish gives an excellent summation of the various proposals for the existence of a long-necked seal by Bernard Heuvelmans, Anthonie Oudemans, and the eighteenth-century doctor James Parsons. Excerpts are below, but I encourage you to read the article in full, and view the images, which can be found at:

https://scienceblogs.com/tetrapodzoology/2008/09/25/ longnecked-seal-described

Based on a number of apparently reliable eyewitness reports, Heuvelmans suggested that this new species, which he dubbed Megalotaria longicollis, was a highly specialised otariid (Otariidae is the group that includes sea lions and fur seals). Giant compared to its relatives (4.5–19 m long), with an elongate, flexible neck and two erectile snorkels that are placed dorsally and in front of the small eyes, it is, he proposed, still capable of terrestrial locomotion but is otherwise the most pelagic of all pinnipeds, having essentially severed the ties that link other pinnipeds to land [adjacent reconstruction of Megalotaria longicollis, Stefano Maugeri].

Heuvelmans wasn't the first to propose the existence of a giant, long-necked pinniped. Oudemans (1892), in his classic The Great Sea-Serpent, identified 'the' sea-serpent (he recognised only a single type) as Megophias megophias, an immense long-necked, long-tailed pinniped belonging to an archaic group (the Longicaudata) that had diverged from all other pinnipeds (grouped together as the Brevicaudata) early on in pinniped evolution. Heuvelmans (1968) was confident that Megophias megophias was a composite creature that combined the traits of several different, distinct giant marine animals (Heuvelmans argued for the presence of nine different types of sea-serpent), and therefore chose to ignore it.

And it occurred to me to be the ideal time to bring to attention the fact that a Long-necked seal was described in the literature long prior to the work of Heuvelmans or even Oudemans. Reporting the observations of a Dr Grew on the Long-necked seal observed 'in diverse countries', James Parsons (1751) included an illustration and description of this pinniped. He described how it was '[M]uch slenderer than either of the former [two other pinnipeds were described earlier in the manuscript]; but that, wherein he principally differs, is the length of his neck; for from his nose-end to his fore-feet, and from thence to his tail, are the same measure; as also in that, instead of his fore-feet, he hath rather fins; not having any claws thereon, as have the other kinds. The head and neck of this species are exactly like those of an otter. One of those, which is also now in our musaeum [sic], taken notice of by the same author, has an head shaped like that of a tortoise; less in proportion than that of every other species, with a narrowness of stricture round the neck: the fore-feet of these are five-finger'd, with nails, like the common seal. Their size, as to the utmost growth of an adult, is also very different. That before described, was 7 feet and an half in length; and, being very young, had scarce any teeth at all' (Parsons 1751, p. 111).

Quite how a pinniped said at first to have a very long neck is then said to have a head and neck 'exactly like those of an otter' I'm not sure, and of course it's not possible to determine whether this 'long-necked seal' has anything to do with Heuvelmans's hypothetical animal of the same name. It's tempting to assume that it was a confused description of a sea lion but, given that Parsons described a specimen 2.3 m long as a juvenile, it still sounds like an interesting animal that we'd like to know more about. To confuse things further, Parsons also mentioned a specimen which 'is but 3 feet long, is very thick in proportion, and has a well-grown set of teeth' (Parsons 1751, p. 112) [adjacent image (not included in *On the Hunt*) shows the creature reportedly seen by J. Mackintosh Bell in the Orkneys, in 1919. It is often regarded as one of the best long-necked seal sightings].

The tantalising possibility remains that the larger specimen would have been significant in zoological terms, but given that we lack data on the provenance and fate of the specimens that were described by Parsons, any further comments would be entirely speculative. James Parsons, 1705–1770, was a British physician who studied medicine in Paris and later worked under James Douglas in London. As yet I haven't done any research on the specimens he studied or wrote about, but this obviously should be done. What happened to his long-necked seal, and what was it?

What indeed? For my money, this is one of the greatest mysteries of cryptozoology and, in fact, biology. Here we have a well-respected doctor, skilled at studying the natural world, documenting a bizarre species of pinniped which perfectly meets descriptions of sea monsters from around the globe – even claiming that specimens had been sent to museums – and yet we have no other mention of these specimens or creatures in any other historic literature. I'd like to volunteer to scour the vault of the Natural History Museum in London! Where are these samples? What was this animal? If it was in fact a long-necked sealion meeting the descriptions above, and was more pelagic than any of its relatives, possibly even giving birth in the water like a manatee or dugong – well, there be sea serpents.

In the reptile section earlier I postulated that the long, flexible neck of Caddy would have evolved to catch fast-moving prey, but is that necessarily true? Could it have evolved for other reasons? Could it aid in sifting through the sediment at the bottom of the ocean like some plesiosaur species are postulated to have done? Or a flamingo? Or a walrus, who use their tusks to disturb the ocean sediment? The silt down there hides all kinds of potential prey species. Could it be diving to eat, then only occasionally surfacing to breathe?

Could a long neck potentially provide a way to lift one's head out of the water to take a breath more easily? This seems like it would only evolve in warmer, more stagnant seas, where the evolutionary advantages outweighed the thermal disadvantages, but who knows? Could a long, flexible neck be used to eat birds? There are many reports of Caddy snapping at birds above and below the surface. Leopard seals have an incredibly flexible neck and eat penguins. Reticulated pythons use their flexible bulk to snag fast-moving birds. Is it possible that a long flexible neck evolved as a feeding strategy? Are we even sure Caddy has a long flexible neck? We certainly are not, but why let that stop the speculation? (Common thinking about plesiosaur necks are that they were actually rigid and their feeding strategy may have been nothing like what I've described above.)

Let's talk pinnipeds under water. Sealions can dive deep (to 600 feet) and swim far (1,000 miles or more), but generally don't dive for long (just a few minutes). Northern elephant seals dive even deeper (to over 2,000 feet) and longer (over 1 hour). Walruses stay on the open ocean for months at a time. It is theoretically plausible to envision a pinniped pushing each of these limits even further.

How about appearance? Google an image of the surfacing northern elephant seal. Soulful eyes? Check. Camel-like lip skin? Check. Flexible head that can stick way out of the water? Yup. A northern elephant seal can pop its head over three feet out of the water. This illustrates that pinnipeds absolutely appear Caddy-like and that Caddy could be a pinniped, but also that "Caddy" can definitely be a mistaken identity for a known pinniped.

Last in this section, I'd like to talk about a very recently extinct marine mammal. Not a pinniped, but a sirenian – the Steller's sea cow. This creature was once common in the North Pacific and its description is quite Caddy-like. It's 30 feet long, has "kind eyes" and a tubular body, lives close to land, is vegetarian and entirely aquatic, and was killed off by people in the mid-eighteenth century. This shows us a few possibilities – could there be a surviving creature similar to this one, that is faster and more adept at avoiding people? Perhaps a deeper-water species? Or, could many of the earliest and native legend Caddy sightings actually be sightings of sea cows?

Either way, I don't think we can rule the pinniped/sirenian out. (Sorry to all of the biologists for grouping these two very different animals together.)

## Cephalopod

Squids and octopuses are weirder than fish. There are also lots of them – 800 extant species, in fact. Most marine biologists will tell you that there are a whole bunch we haven't identified yet, especially in the deep ocean and the coldest waters. They are massive too – giant squid, colossal squid, ubermega squid... okay, I made that last one up – again, but it's only a matter of time until we find one. We're talking about animals that are reported to reach sizes between 45 and 60 feet, maybe bigger, and we've just started positively identifying them in the last two decades. The first images of a live giant squid were in 2004, and one wasn't filmed until 2012. Reports of these beasts go back as far as people have been on the water. These are enormous and mysterious deep-sea predators.

Cephalopods are smart. They can problem-solve, swim mazes, and demonstrate signs of cognition. They grow to monstrous sizes in a very short time. The giant squid grows from a few inches to thirty feet in just a few years. We know next to nothing about their behaviors, migrations, mating habits, hunting strategies, etc. There is the potential to discover dozens of new species as we get more adept at exploring the deepest reaches of the oceans.

Checking the boxes, these meet all of the criteria for being mistaken for Caddy. They also present great potential for actually *being* Caddy, meaning a bizarre-looking giant squid might be the creature that people are seeing. Squid, octopus, nautilus, and cuttlefish morphology is varied and bizarre. Telescope, vampire, long-armed, arm-thrower, flap-jack, and dumbo are just a few of the common names for some of the odder cephalopods out there.

These animals are rarely seen alive, but dead they tend to draw a crowd, as well as a crowd of birds and other sea life anxious to feed on the giant carcasses. Dying squid will flail their massive arms around, as seen in the Japanese footage of a colossal squid snared by a fishing line. Could the sightings of Caddy "hunting" birds actually be a dead or dying giant squid being mobbed by sea birds? Dolphins are known to mob troublesome animals as well – even sharks. Could this account for some sightings? A pod of dolphins, killer whales, other cetaceans, sealions, etc., attacking, playing with, or simply swimming near a giant squid or large octopus?

Squid and octopus are huge, weird, smart, dangerous, and live all over the place. How, you might be asking, could someone mistake one for a sea serpent? Quite easily, actually. Imagine a large squid, like a giant squid, for instance, on the surface of the water. Imagine one of its huge, grasping, hunting tentacles sticking out of the water. Imagine that tentacle trying to grab a seagull – as the giant pacific octopus has been videotaped doing (in British Columbia, actually). Does this massive tentacle with a pyramid-shaped grasper at the end look like the neck and head of a sea serpent? Damn right it does. Could Caddy actually be hunting sea birds? Certainly, yes. But that sea serpent could very easily be a squid.

## Deer/moose/bird

Let's rule this out as a possible Caddy candidate right away – as in, Caddy is not a new species of deer, moose, or bird. However, I bet some Caddy sightings are a mistaken identity for any of these three. Moose have been known to swim around 15 miles and will dive over 15 feet underwater in search of tasty plants on lake and river bottoms. Moose and deer have occasionally taken a dip in saltwater channels as well. It's notoriously hard to judge size on the water, and an albatross (native to BC) is pretty big and commonly found around sealions, seals, orcas, porpoises, and many other marine animals who can create the classic "hump in the water," while the bird produces the "horse-shaped head." They sometimes try to eat the same thing as the bigger marine animal, sometimes pieces of what the marine animal leaves behind, and sometimes the dead marine animal itself. Sometimes they are investigating, or just happen to be in the same place.

I've been in the water with swimming moose and it is *freaky*. When a moose pops its head out of the water it looks pretty unnatural, and unless you know what you're looking at it would be easy to jump to conclusions about all kinds of mystery creatures. Bull Moose and deer in BC shed their antlers every year in the winter and regrow them in the spring, and thus wouldn't have them when most Caddy sightings occur. There's also a rare phenomenon called "devil's antlers," which occurs when a moose becomes castrated. After this horrifying event, a moose drops its current antlers and immediately begins growing a deformed pair, which it will keep for the rest of its life. These deformed antlers could explain some of the knobbly appendages reported on Caddy's head.

## Here's what I HOPE Caddy is, but for which I have absolutely no supporting evidence – and, actually, find it very unlikely

Let's quickly talk about the evolution of marine mammals. Cetaceans started as land-dwelling even-toed undulates – pig/camel/deer/sheep/goat/cows/giraffe-like creatures – before making their way to the sea. Pinnipeds likely (although there is still some dispute) share a common bear-raccoon-like ancestor. Let's focus on cetaceans.

This ancestral creature was clearly adaptable, radiating into all of the diverse life mentioned above. The evolution into cetaceans appears to have occurred in India about 50 million years ago (again, there are disputes about this – some evidence from Antarctica moves this to 5 million years). Could the creature which eventually became a giraffe also have spawned an aquatic beast?

It clearly had the potential for an elongated neck, and all members of the giraffe family (extant and extinct) have knobbly horns called ossicones. These are unique features – not horns or antlers – and only appear in giraffes and okapis, but show up in fossil evidence of all species in this line. Caddy is often reported to have a "giraffe-like face" and "giraffe-like knobbly horns" – could Caddy be related to giraffes?

It's a stretch (pun intended), and I have no evidence for this, but it would be fun! As shown above, a long neck would be just as useful in the ocean as it is on land – you could sift around on the bottom and fish out all the tasty tunicates and worms down there without your bulky body kicking up too much muck. Also, Caddy is sometimes reported to be herbivorous, being seen with mouthfuls of seaweed. No cetacean is – but giraffes are! I know, I know, there's no evidence, but it's an interesting theory.

## I made a chart. Because, Science!

Looking at all the above information, I thought it would be helpful to organize it into a chart, which can help us see if there could be a mistaken identity for a known species in one of our "target" groups by using the two most frequently cited candidates from each. This gets surprisingly tricky when talking about head and body size and shape because eyewitness accounts are so notoriously unreliable. I'm going to use my own judgment here and make a call like, "I don't think anyone seeing a loon would mistake it for Caddy's head, but seeing a group of loons from a great distance away swimming together in a current could look like the body of a long undulating creature." I'll note when I'm talking about a group of animals rather than a single individual. The more checks, the more likely that mistaken identity is a potential – especially if "British Columbia" is also checked. While "out of place" animals happen all the time, I dare say a tropical sea snake is not a candidate for mistaken identity in BC's waters. They have, on rare occasions, been brought into California's waters on a bizarre current, but have never made it north of the US border into the truly cold waters of BC.

I'll also carry down the traits of the individual species into a larger grouping like "reptile" to show the potential for Caddy to be a new type of this group. The more checked boxes indicating a prevalence of this trait in a grouping of species, the more likely Caddy might be a new species of this group. They only get the "X" if there is no qualifier with it for this one – this way, we can distinguish between a possible mistaken identity for only seeing part of a known animal, and the actual potential for a new member of the group.

I hope this all makes sense – either way, onto the chart!

| Animal | British Columbia | Majority of life in Deep water | Reproduces in water | > 6ft at largest point | Camel shaped head | Tube-like body Shape | Could appear as a hump in the water | "Up/down" undulation or "head-up" swimming |
|---|---|---|---|---|---|---|---|---|
| Leatherback | X | | | X | | | X | X |
| Sea Snake | | | X | X | | X | X ① | ① |
| **REPTILE** | X | | X | X | | X | X | X |
| Beaked Whale | X | X ② | X | X | | | X | X ⑤ |
| Toothed whales/porpoise | X | | X | X ③ | | | X | X ⑤ |
| **CETACEAN** | X | | X | X | | | X | X |
| Manatee | | | X | X | X | X | X | X |
| Elephant Seal | X | X ② | | X | X | X | X | X |
| **OTHER MARINE MAMMAL** | X | | X | X | X | X | X | X |
| Eel | X | X | X | X | | X | X | X |
| Oarfish | X | X | X | X | | X | X | X ⑥ |
| **BONY FISH** | X | X | X | X | | X | X | |
| Frilled | X | X | X | X | | X | X | |
| Sleeper | X | X | X | X | | | X | |
| **SHARK** | X | X | X | X | | X | X | X |
| Squid | X | X | X | X | X ④ | X ④ | X | X ④ |
| Octopus | X | X | X | X | X ④ | X ④ | X | X ④ |
| **CEPHALOPOD** | X | X | X | X ⑤ | X | X | X | X ④ |
| Albatross | X | | | X ⑤ | | | | |
| Gull | X | | | X ⑤ | | | | |
| **BIRD** | X | | | | | | | |
| Deer | X | | | X | X | | X | X |
| Moose | X | | | X | X | | X | X |
| **CERVIDAE** | X | | | X | X | X | X | X |
| Salamander | X | | X | X | | X | X | |
| Caelian | | | X | | | X | X | |
| **Amphibian** | X | | X | X | | X | X | |

① No "up/down" motion/no known sea snake is large/thick enough for its body to produce the described "hump."

② Frequent, long, and deep dives.

③ Pods even larger.

④ Tentacle sticking out of the water:

I know I said no qualifiers get Xs, but this is technically not a qualifier as the individual animal does display the characteristic. This is an explanation of how I reached it – a tentacle above the water does show the head shape associated with Caddy and can appear to undulate or stay fixed.

⑤ In a group – can appear very serpentine in a group, with waves/water motion:

I am aware that an albatross's wingspan is greater than 6 feet and it therefore meets the criteria of being "larger than 6 feet at the largest point," their head is approximately the right shape, etc., but I'm using my own judgment in saying that an individual bird with its wings spread will not be confused with a sea serpent.

⑥ Oarfish only surface when they are dying and often are floating on their sides. They are described as "rippling" and "undulating," but on its side, the "side to side" motion of a fish becomes "up and down."

## *Finally*, the chart gets us to what I think is most likely

According to my chart, the most likely explanation for an unknown animal that:

1. is found in British Columbia,
2. spends the majority of its life in deep water,
3. does not come on land to reproduce,
4. is longer than six feet,
5. has what appears to be a camel-shaped head (or appendage) which is sometimes visible sticking out of the water,
6. has a tube-like body (or visible appendage), and
7. appears to swim in an undulating "up-down" manner or stick its camel-like head out of the water.

Is…

(Drum roll please)

With a perfect score of eight checks…

A cephalopod. *Wha-whaaaa* (sad trombone noise). I almost called this chapter "The cryptid you'll be the least excited about when we find it." Not me though, I love squid – I can't wait for us to find some new ridiculous bastards.

The next most likely is a pinniped/sirenian with seven checks (I left the penis theory out of the chart), then a shark or bony fish with six checks each, followed by a cetacean, reptile, and, surprisingly, a cervidae with five checks, then an amphibian with four, and last a bird, with one lonely check.

The real science behind these "large undiscovered animals" in the oceans touted by even the most conservative marine biologists is far less sexy than it sounds. They mean new species, but not new monsters. Like, a new species of seal will probably look very, very close to a known species, to the point where tons of people have seen it but thought it was the already named species. Genetic testing will show otherwise – it is a new species, but a new *sad trombone* species. The same can be said of whales. Sure, we're likely to find a new species of whale – probably a beaked whale – but it will probably look a lot like other species of beaked whales. When you hear "new species of whale discovered in 2017," it's easy to think, "Wow! A whale! The ocean is so mysterious!" And you're right, but that new whale doesn't prove it. Take a look at it. It probably doesn't have tusks, or a Mohawk made of bony protrusions, or even an extra few flippers somewhere on its body. It probably looks a hell of a lot like another species of whale. New species of squid and shark are really the most exciting because, as non-air breathers, there really is a good chance we've never seen anything like them. The deep oceans are where "real" undiscovered monsters could be. "Caddy" may not exist, but I'm certain Caddy does. I'm certain, as are most scientists, that there is a large, unknown animal in the deep oceans that at least occasionally shows up in British Columbia.

So, a squid or octopus is a likely candidate for a sea serpent. This poses some issues with ever "actually" identifying Caddy, because if we find a new species of squid that hangs out in BC, the public will say, "Cool! A new squid!" then immediately go back to watching sports-ball. No one will say, "Cool! A sea serpent!" This is an issue in cryptozoology in the modern era. Unless you find the animal as it appears in the myth, you haven't found the animal. Take the Yeti. Harry Marshall found hairs from a Polar Bear in Bhutan. Polar bears don't live in Bhutan. It was a blip on the news, but it was a blip about a bear being discovered where a bear is not known to live, not a "Yeti" being discovered. Despite clearly offering an explanation for the Yeti, it wasn't an abominable snowman/hairy hominid, and therefore the Yeti is still a mystery. Same would go for a squid discovery in BC.

This is one of the main problems with trying to talk about "Caddy" as if it's a "real" animal – in fact, any cryptid faces the same issue. How can we say "misidentification" when we don't have a positive identification to compare with? You can definitely say a report of a mountain lion that, upon review of the cellphone video, turns out to be a housecat was a misidentification, but how can we say a sighting that seems to be a large squid is a "misidentification" of a Caddy? Maybe it's a positive identification – maybe Caddy is a squid. Maybe that's just as exciting! Maybe, instead of being disappointed, we could be amazed that there is a deep-sea squid species that seems to have a penchant for hunting at the surface and calls the BC waters its home! That's exciting and interesting stuff! See, without a reference standard, any "Caddy" sighting isn't a "Caddy" sighting – it's the sighting of an animal that the witness can't immediately identify.

We can look at the time of year of the sighting, the location, the habitat, what else is happening in the area, the description of the physical appearance, and the behavior of the animal, then compare that to what we know about known species and narrow down the list of possibilities. We can then make a likely ID which we can be fairly certain is the animal they spotted. The only reason to jump to "unknown" is when something about the sighting directly goes against what we know about the known species that could possibly be in the area. Even if some aspect of the sighting is "weird," if it's within the range of possibility it's still much more likely to be a known animal than a new one. The "seals aren't in the bay at that time of year" argument doesn't rule out there being a sick seal or one acting weird every now and then. "Bears don't normally walk on two legs" doesn't rule out a bear with an injury causing it to walk primarily upright (as one bear did in NJ neighborhoods for years). On the spectrum of possibilities, it is more likely that, occasionally, people see a moose swimming near a pod of porpoises, or a frilled shark has turned up, than the likelihood that a very large, completely unique type of reptile, amphibian, or mammal is in the waters of BC. If we talk about a new species of cephalopod or fish, the scales start to, if not tip towards "likely," then at least balance out a little. There is far less of a jump in thinking that they could go without a positive ID for so long.

The chart also shows us how likely misidentification is – how a swimming moose, at a distance, can look like a sea serpent's head. How the hump of a leatherback or beaked whale looks like the hump of a sea serpent. Group some of these together – say, a moose surrounded by a curious pod of porpoises – and you get an even more likely misidentification (combine the checks for each animal and you get a perfect score of 8). Of the animals we looked at, the ones most likely to be identified as Caddy are a squid or an octopus with 8 checks each, followed by an oarfish with 7 – which also makes sense as the historic "ah ha" behind sea serpent sightings – and a manatee, should it find its way into BC waters, also with 7. Followed by a beaked whale, elephant seal, eel, and frilled shark with 6 checks. A toothed whale, sleeper shark, deer, and moose all get a respectable 5. A salamander, Caelian, leatherback, and sea snake all receive an abysmal 3. (Which seems very wrong as a sea snake *is* literally a sea serpent, but the chart doesn't lie. A serpent in the sea is among the *least* likely animals to be mistaken as a sea serpent. A deer is more likely to be mistaken for a sea serpent as an actual sea serpent. That's why data is important – even pretty sketchy data like this. Wow. I went to college.) And finally, birds are the least likely to be mistaken for a sea serpent with only 2 checks each. I will listen to disagreements to this that come in chart form only.

Might Caddy be some bizarre elongated squid with a modified tentacle that looks like a horse's head? Yup. Might it also be some super weird new massive reptile species with a weird body shape? A new species of fish or something entirely unique, something we'll have trouble classifying, like a hagfish? Yes, it could. I think, personally, that it's likely a species of deep-sea squid, shark, octopus, or bony fish that has evolved to feed closer to the surface during certain times of the year than it normally does, and once in a while we get a glimpse of it. I also think the vast majority of the sightings are misidentification of a known, or combination of known, animals. I do think there is a large animal living in the deep ocean off the BC coast, but I also think that, when we find it, most people won't call it "Caddy," and that's a shame.

I think what the chart and the preceding discussion show is that there are tons of *possibilities* for what Caddy could be. We have examples that show it *could* be an amphibian that has gone further down the evolutionary path of a tiger salamander and gotten larger than a giant Chinese salamander. It *could* be a reptile that is generating body heat like a loggerhead and giving live birth like a sea snake. It *could* be a pinniped with an elongated neck that breeds on some uncharted island or has evolved a water-birth strategy, like a manatee. It *could* be many of the other types of animals mentioned – the marine environment is weird, biology is weird, and marine biology is just bizarre and produces spectacularly peculiar adaptations. While it *could* be many different types of animal, history, biology, and chemistry tell us that it is *likely* a cephalopod, a bony fish, or a shark. The platypus isn't a likely thing, yet there it is – an egg-laying mammal, happily using its weird bill and electrolocation to dig through the mud looking for worms and its venomous spur to fight off would-be attackers. That's what makes biology so much fun.

So maybe Caddy is really a giant, ridiculous marine skink that breathes through its butt, generates body heat by constantly treading water, gives live birth, eats tiny fish all day, has super concentrated, ion-rich urea and hemoglobin-deprived blood, and lives for hundreds of years, thereby accounting for very small numbers in a breeding population. Because screw it – why not? And how cool and biologically interesting would that be? Life in the ocean doesn't always make logical sense.

# Acknowledgements

While I have dedicated this book to my parents, I truly could not have completed it without the help of many incredible people who I am so fortunate to have in my life. I'd like to take a minute to thank each of them.

Anna – my phenomenal wife. She not only joins me on many adventures, but has put up with all of the insanity that comes with being a partner to a guy who does all of the stuff described in here.

Our kids, Luna Caulfield and Wallace Charles. The greatest aspect of my life is being a part of theirs.

My insane and wonderful family – Al, Mom, Sarah, and Nathan who have supported and encouraged me throughout my life. Mom, who learned more about alligator reproduction than she probably ever wanted to in her quest to support a budding young biologist and Al who took me camping and fishing despite having no interest in these activities himself, which I never knew until I was in my late twenties. Sorry about child welfare having to come to the house and watch you change diapers and question Sarah about possible neglect/abuse after I got salmonella from a lizard, then spread it to about a dozen friends, and cracked my head open sledding, and sliced my legs open sliding down a hill to catch a snake – hopefully this makes up for the embarrassment?

The entire current and past Icon family, particularly Harry and Laura Marshall. Harry and Laura are two of my favorite people on Earth. They are the people Anna and I want to be when we grow up. They are the smartest, nicest, funniest, and most caring and loving people you could hope to meet, and the greatest thing about doing TV has been having them enter our lives. We love them like family. In addition to Harry and Laura there's Andie Clare, Lucy Middleboe, Stephen McQuillan,

Barny Revill, James Bickersteth, Alex Holden, Anna Gol, Ben Roy, Laura Coates, Sol Welch, Belinda Partridge, Abi Wrigley, Duncan Fairs, Robin Cox, Simon Reay, Brendan McGinty, and everyone else, who continue to be amazing forces of encouragement and support.

The Nat Geo team behind *Beast Hunter* – Janet Han Vissering, Steve Burns, Ashley Hoppin, Sydney Suissa, Russel Howard, Chris Albert, Geoff Daniels, Mike Mavretic, Dara Klatt, Steve Ashworth, Whit Higgins, and others. Thank you so much for your support and trust in allowing me to fulfill a lifelong dream, and letting Icon take the lead and make a series we are all really proud of.

The most amazing and supportive group of friends I could ask for – Adam Manning, Dom Pellegrino, Joe Viola, and Adrianna Wooden. Thank you for sticking by me and being there for me and my family through everything.

Thank you so much to the entire team at John Hunt Publishing, especially John Hunt, who saw the potential of the massive and messy manuscript I sent over, Dominic James, who assured all of my insecurities and answered all of my questions while reassuring me that it was all going to be okay, and the expert editing of Graham Clarke, who managed to pull these six books together and make them the cohesive series.

My very literary friends and family who served as the first reviewers of this book – Anna Spain, Al Spain, Joe Viola, Dom Pellegrino, Richard Sugg, Sarah Franchi, Gene Campbell, Tim Fogarty, John Johnson, Zeb Schobernd, Sarahbeth Golden, and Luke Kirkland – thank you for your insights and mocking. This book is much better because of you.

The folks at my day job who have supported my insane extracurricular activities – especially Bill O'Connor who gave me the opportunity to do this and assured me I'd still have a job when I returned.

Thanks to all of the incredible fixers, guides, and translators who kept us alive and safe, often risking your own lives in the process.

Thanks, finally, to the readers and fans of these shows! I hope you've enjoyed what you've seen and read! You can find all of my social media stuff at www.patspain.com. I'll try to answer questions and respond as best I can. Genuinely – thank you!

**Continue the adventure with the Pat Spain On the Hunt Series**

**A Little Bigfoot: On the Hunt in Sumatra**
Pat Spain lost a layer of skin, pulled leeches off his neither
regions and was violated by an Orangutan for this book
Paperback: 978-1-78904-605-2
ebook: 978-1-78904-606-9

**200,000 Snakes: On the Hunt in Manitoba**
Pat Spain got and lost his dream job, survived stage 3 cancer,
and laid down in a pit of 200,000 snakes for this book.
Paperback: 978-1-78904-648-9
ebook: 978-1-78904-649-6

**A Living Dinosaur: On the Hunt in West Africa**
Pat Spain was nearly thrown in a Cameroonian prison, learned
to use a long-drop toilet while a village of pygmy children
watched, and was deemed "too dirty to fly" for this book.
Paperback: 978-1-78904-656-4
ebook: 978-1-78904-657-1

**A Bulletproof Ground Sloth: On the Hunt in Brazil**
Pat Spain participated in the most extreme tribal ritual,
accidentally smuggled weapons, and almost lost his mind in the
Amazonian rainforest for this book.
Paperback: 978-1-78904-652-6
ebook: 978-1-78904-653-3

**The Mongolian Death Worm: On the Hunt in the Gobi Desert**
Pat Spain ingested toxic "foods", made a name for himself in
traditional Mongolian wrestling, and experienced the worst
bathroom on Earth for this book.
Paperback: 978-1-78904-650-2
ebook: 978-1-78904-651-9

**Sea Serpents: On the Hunt in British Columbia**
Pat Spain went to the bottom of the ocean, triggered a bunch of
very angry fisherman, and attempted to recreate an iconic scene
from Apocalypse Now for this book.

Paperback: 978-1-78904-654-0
ebook: 978-1-78904-655-7

# Recent bestsellers from 6th Books are:

## The Afterlife Unveiled
What the Dead Are Telling us About Their World!
Stafford Betty
What happens after we die? Spirits speaking through mediums
know, and they want us to know. This book unveils their world...
Paperback: 978-1-84694-496-3 ebook: 978-1-84694-926-5

## Spirit Release
Sue Allen
A guide to psychic attack, curses, witchcraft, spirit attachment,
possession, soul retrieval, haunting, deliverance, exorcism and
more, as taught at the College of Psychic Studies.
Paperback: 978-1-84694-033-0 ebook: 978-1-84694-651-6

## I'm Still With You
True Stories of Healing Grief Through Spirit Communication
Carole J. Obley
A series of after-death spirit communications which uplift, comfort
and heal, and show how love helps us grieve.
Paperback: 978-1-84694-107-8 ebook: 978-1-84694-639-4

## Less Incomplete
A Guide to Experiencing the Human Condition Beyond the
Physical Body
Sandie Gustus
Based on 40 years of scientific research, this book is a dynamic
guide to understanding life beyond the physical body.
Paperback: 978-1-84694-351-5 ebook: 978-1-84694-892-3

## Advanced Psychic Development
Becky Walsh
Learn how to practise as a professional, contemporary spiritual medium.
Paperback: 978-1-84694-062-0 ebook: 978-1-78099-941-8


## Astral Projection Made Easy
and overcoming the fear of death
Stephanie June Sorrell
From the popular Made Easy series, *Astral Projection Made Easy* helps to eliminate the fear of death, through discussion of life beyond the physical body.
Paperback: 978-1-84694-611-0 ebook: 978-1-78099-225-9


## The Miracle Workers Handbook
Seven Levels of Power and Manifestation of the Virgin Mary
Sherrie Dillard
Learn how to invoke the Virgin Mary's presence, communicate with her, receive her grace and miracles and become a miracle worker.
Paperback: 978-1-84694-920-3 ebook: 978-1-84694-921-0


## Divine Guidance
The Answers You Need to Make Miracles
Stephanie J. King
Ask any question and the answer will be presented, like a direct line to higher realms... *Divine Guidance* helps you to regain control over your own journey through life.
Paperback: 978-1-78099-794-0 ebook: 978-1-78099-793-3

# The End of Death
How Near-Death Experiences Prove the Afterlife
Admir Serrano
A compelling examination of the phenomena of Near-Death
Experiences.
Paperback: 978-1-78279-233-8 ebook: 978-1-78279-232-1

# Where After
Mariel Forde Clarke
A journey that will compel readers to view life after death in a
completely different way.
Paperback: 978-1-78904-617-5 ebook: 978-1-78904-618-2

# Harvest: The True Story of Alien Abduction
G L Davies
G. L. Davies's most terrifying investigation yet reveals one
woman's terrifying ordeal of alien visitation, nightmarish visions
and a prophecy of destruction on a scale never before seen in
Pembrokeshire's peaceful history.
Paperback: 978-1-78904-385-3 ebook: 978-1-78904-386-0

# The Scars of Eden
Paul Wallis
How do we distinguish between our ancestors' ideas of God and
close encounters of an extra-terrestrial kind?
Paperback: 978-1-78904-852-0 ebook: 978-1-78904-853-7

Readers of ebooks can buy or view any of these bestsellers by clicking on the live link in the title. Most titles are published in paperback and as an ebook. Paperbacks are available in traditional bookshops. Both print and ebook formats are available online.

Find more titles and sign up to our readers' newsletter at http://www.johnhuntpublishing.com/mind-body-spirit.

Follow us on Facebook at https://www.facebook.com/OBooks and Twitter at https://twitter.com/obooks.